BY THE EDITORS OF
CONSUMER GUIDE®

WALKING

for Health & Fitness

PUBLICATIONS INTERNATIONAL, LTD.

Louis Weber, C.E.O
Publications International, Ltd.
7373 North Cicero Avenue
Lincolnwood, Illinois 60646

Permission is never granted for commercial purposes.

Manufactured in Yugoslavia, by Zrinski,
h g f e d c b a

ISBN: 0-88176-496-5

Library of Congress Catalog Card Number: 88–61665

Contributing Writer: Rebecca Hughes

Consultant: Michael Pollock, Ph.D., exercise physiologist and director of the Center for Exercise Science at the University of Florida.

NOTE: Neither the Editors of CONSUMER GUIDE® and Publications International, Ltd., nor the writers, consultant, or publisher take responsibility for any possible consequences from any program, treatment, procedure, test, or action by any person reading or following the information in this book. The publisher advises the reader to check with a physician before beginning any exercise program. Every effort has been made to assure that the information in this book is accurate and current at the time of printing.

TABLE OF CONTENTS

FROM HERE TO THERE

When you think about it, what is walking? Well, it's a way to get from where you are now to where you want to be—when there's no car, bus, train, or elevator that can take you. Walking, however, is more than a means of getting from one *location* to another. It's a way to get from the shape you're in now to the healthy, fit shape you want to be in. Be assured, there's no vehicle that can get you there as safely and easily.

Walking can help you attain that trim figure you've been "dieting" to have. It allows you to burn off fat without losing muscle and without depriving your body of the essential nutrients it needs. And it can help tone your muscles and shape up your legs.

Brisk walking is an aerobic exercise; it can train your heart, lungs, and muscles to work more efficiently. As they're conditioned, they'll require less oxygen to do the same amount of work. And that can translate into less strain on your heart and a lower risk of heart disease for you.

Studies have shown that weight-bearing exercise like walking can strengthen your bones and help ward off osteoporosis, the bone-thinning disease that strikes so many older women. A walking program can help arthritics to maintain flexibility in their affected joints. Regular walking can also play a role in keeping your digestive tract running smoothly.

Frequent walks can help boost your energy and make getting started in the morning easier. Walking can help you feel better, calmer, and less stressed. Doctors are even "prescribing" walking as a treatment for depression.

You may have heard similar claims made for other aerobic exercises. But consider this: The only exercise that will do you any good is the exercise you do. And walking is easy—as easy as putting one foot in front of the other. Indeed, as a form of exercise, walking has one of the lowest dropout rates around. Walking doesn't require great expertise, perfect technique, or lots of athletic ability. But you've probably realized that already. You've been walking since you were a baby.

Walking is inexpensive. It doesn't require loads of heavy-duty equipment. As a matter of fact, a good pair of walking shoes and a watch are probably the only equipment you'll need. Walking is also convenient. You can walk in the morning, in the evening, on your way to work, or even on your lunch hour. You can walk alone or with your family, friends, or coworkers.

One of the best features of walking for health and fitness, however, is its unbeatable safety record. Walking can be intense enough to boost your aerobic capacity and your overall health, but it's also low-impact. That means it's easy on your joints and safe for people of all ages and fitness levels. If you've been inactive for a long time, walking can safely help you increase your fitness. If you've suffered injuries doing other types of exercise, walking can help you get back on your feet and back into shape. Walking is even used as a way to move heart attack victims down the road of recovery.

If you think that walking is just for wimps, though, think again. Walking can help even the most fit people maintain and increase their fitness. By stepping up the pace of their walks or walking with weights, athletes can boost the aerobic fitness benefits of walking to those of a jog, without greatly increasing the risk of injury.

This book outlines the health and fitness benefits of walking and provides you with the information you need to walk safely and efficiently. You'll find discussions of how walking can help you lose weight, increase your aerobic fitness, fight off heart disease and other health problems, and feel more energetic and less tense.

We show you how to prepare your body for a walking program—including tips on making healthy changes in your diet, checking out your health before you hit the road, and preparing for all kinds of weather. You'll also learn how you can use your heart rate as a guide to exercise intensity.

You'll also find the CONSUMER GUIDE® Walking Programs, complete with simple guidelines and handy charts. These programs have been designed to get you walking and keep you going down the road to fitness, no matter what kind of shape you're in now.

The starter programs allow you to walk at a comfortable pace as you get your body ready for more vigorous exercise. By starting out slowly and progressing gradually, you'll be much less likely to injure yourself and become discouraged—and much more likely to stay with your walking program for life.

Once you have mastered the starter programs, you'll advance to the basic walking program. It will give you a hearty (and heart-healthy) workout that can build your aerobic fitness. With this program, you can even adjust the intensity of your walks and the amount of time you spend on each walk to suit your goals and your schedule.

Even if you've recently suffered a heart attack, you'll find two suggested walking programs that you can discuss with your doctor. Chances are, your doctor will permit you to try one of these programs to help you get back on your feet.

One of walking's major advantages is that it can be as flexible as you are. You can make your walking workouts as strenuous as you like. Plain old freestyle walking can be an end in itself—or a stepping stone to more vigorous walking workouts. If you want more of a challenge, you'll find chapters on racewalking, walking with weights, and hiking that will show you how to enhance the aerobic benefits you get from walking, boost the intensity of your workouts, and burn more calories.

We recognize that the key to reaping health and fitness benefits from any exercise program is sticking with it for a lifetime. We also realize that unless an exercise is enjoyable, flexible, and convenient, your chances of staying with it for the rest of your life may not be all that good. So we've included chapters designed to keep you from becoming an exercise dropout. In these sections, you'll find tips on finding pleasant places to walk no matter where you live. You'll find tips on fitting fitness into a hectic schedule. You'll also find suggestions for adding a little "spice" to your walking routine.

While walking is a low-impact activity, you still need to know what to do in case you experience discomfort. So we've included a chapter on coping with discomfort. It's essential reading before you hit the road.

This book provides you with all you need to know to turn walking into an exercise tool—a way to improve your fitness and increase your health. Of course, you still have to take the first step. You need to make the all-important decision to begin. Once you've read through this book, the decision shouldn't be a difficult one to make. You'll see for yourself that the benefits of a lifelong walking program far outweigh any excuses you may have developed over the years for not exercising. It's tough to find a simpler, more enjoyable way to do so much for yourself—and get from where you are now to where you want to be.

Chapter 1

WALK INTO SHAPE

Has the "no pain, no gain" theory of exercise chased you back to your easy chair? Are you wondering why something that's supposed to be so good for you has to be so uncomfortable and inconvenient? Take heart! Many exercise scientists stress that the key to reaping the health and fitness benefits of physical activity is to disregard the "no pain, no gain" myth and instead choose a regular, moderate exercise program that you can stick with for life. After all, an exercise program won't do you much good if you don't follow it.

So what do you choose? Why not pick the activity that you've been doing all your life? Walking, our natural means of getting from one place to another, is the number one lifelong activity—providing health and fitness gains without all that pain. Because of its unbeatable convenience and safety, this low-impact activity has one of the lowest dropout rates of any form of exercise.

Indeed, when scientists first investigated the health and fitness benefits of exercise, it was walking, not running, that they studied. Now, as walking is "rediscovered" and gains new respect, it is becoming more and more popular as a means to lose and control weight, tone muscles, build strength and endurance, and increase aerobic capacity.

Weight Loss and Control

People in search of that lean, healthy look have gone on countless crash diets and lost mountains of fat—only to gain it back again. They've all but starved themselves for the sake of a slim body, only to find themselves on the roller coaster of weight gain. A series of crash diets, devoid of exercise, strip the body of needed water and muscle, in addition to fat. The fat returns in a flash when the dieting stops, yet only physical activity can rebuild the muscle. The body is left with a lower metabolic rate and a higher risk of future weight gain.

How do you get off this roller coaster? After years of study of what works—and what doesn't—in weight loss and control, the experts seem to have come to some agreement. They now favor lifelong, consistent changes in eating and exercise habits, instead of short-term diets and exercise binges. This lasting weight loss cannot happen overnight; it demands a lifetime commitment. But the result is a sustained increase in the body's percentage of lean body mass (muscle and bone), and a decrease in the percentage of fat.

The body usually maintains a delicate balance between the calories taken in as food and those burned up as "fuel." For instance, consuming 2,400 calories of food in a day and burning up 2,400 calories by sleeping, eating, walking, and performing other activities results in neither weight loss nor weight gain. However, if there are any calories left over—if, for example, you take in 2,400 calories and burn only 2,300, leaving 100 extra—they are stored for a metabolic "rainy day" as fat. Storing 3,500 of these extra calories gives you 1 pound of fat. To lose weight, you must use more calories than you consume—by eating fewer calories, by exercising, or, as the experts advise, by combining the two.

When you diet without exercising, your body reacts as if it were being starved. It lowers its metabolic rate and cuts down its energy expenditure. In other words, your body burns fewer calories in order to maintain its "setpoint"—the weight that its metabolic controls consider healthy and normal. This was a very useful mechanism during times of famine, because it enabled the individual to survive when less food was available. But it's the exact opposite of what a dieter wants. The dieter needs to burn more calories to shed unwanted fat.

What's more, inactivity can help lead to obesity (defined as weighing 20 percent more than average for your build). People who are obese, in turn, tend to become less active. This compounds their weight problem, completing a vicious circle in which stress, anxiety, and tension lead to compulsive eating, which shows up as fat; that extra fat further contributes to inactivity, which begets more weight gain—causing even greater stress, anxiety, and tension.

As mentioned earlier, dieting without exercising also tends to rob the body of lean muscle tissue and water. (Weakness and dark, strong-smelling urine are signs of this muscle wasting.) But the body needs a certain amount of water to avoid dehydration. So when you replenish the water, some of the weight that was lost at the start of the diet is gained back. However, the lean muscle tissue, which contributes to a fit and trim appearance, can only be regained through physical activity.

Regular exercise, especially when combined with modest changes in diet, can help you break the vicious circle of weight gain. And a variety of responsible weight loss programs are spreading the message. They now prescribe exercise along with diets, to fight fat gradually—and for keeps. In one popular program, for example, members can choose either walking or stair climbing. Together with a specially designed food plan, the exercise improves body shape by encouraging fat loss from major flab-collecting areas (hips, thighs, buttocks, and abdomen).

Walking, as a lifelong activity with one of the lowest dropout rates, is especially well-suited to play the starring role in the exercise side of the food-and-exercise equation. As a sustained, rhythmic workout, walking conserves and even builds muscle while it burns calories. And muscle keeps busy, with a higher metabolic rate than fat. So the more muscle and the less fat you have, the more calories you burn while resting.

What about the old myth that exercise defeats the purpose of weight loss because it increases your appetite and makes you eat more? Well, the experts still don't agree on the relationship between appetite and exercise. Several studies suggest, however, that appetite may actually decrease in very sedentary people who begin moderate exercise programs. The important point to remember, however, is that walking burns calories without lowering your resting metabolic rate the way dieting does. By burning calories through exercise, you won't need to make such severe changes in your diet. That doesn't mean you can eat anything you want. But you'll be able to eat a balanced diet that includes regular meals and enough nutrients to build and maintain a healthy body. You won't have to starve yourself.

In addition, people who become more active tend to change their food choices spontaneously in a healthier direction, opting for a better-balanced diet with less saturated fat and total calories and more fiber and fresh foods, according to Rose E. Frisch, Ph.D., associate professor of population sciences at the Harvard School of Public Health. Since obesity and unhealthy eating habits are risk factors for coronary heart disease (see Chapter 2), a key side benefit of walking is a lowered risk of heart disease.

Just how many calories does walking burn? In general, a 150-pound person walking at average speed (from two to three-and-a-half miles per hour) can count on burning about 80 calories a mile. (This amount rises with your weight, your speed, and the shortness of your legs. A 200-pound person burns about one-third more calories, and a 100-pounder about one-third fewer, than a 150-pound person.) So a brisk walk, covering three-and-a-half miles in an hour, burns about 280 calories. When repeated each day, this excellent habit burns about 3900 calories—more than a pound of fat—every 2 weeks.

This rate of weight loss is a far cry from the "pound-a-day" claims of the crash diets. But when combined with sensible eating habits—a balanced diet with smaller portion sizes and fewer fats, sweets, and high-calorie foods—a walking program can soon translate into a better-looking and healthier figure. Research has shown that weight losses in this moderate range, of one or two pounds of fat a week, are the ones that last. In contrast, higher loss rates tend to involve losses of water and lean muscle, as well as body fat.

If you are out-of-shape or overweight, you should follow a "go-slow" approach when you begin your exercise program. This is a hard lesson to learn, especially if you are a competitive person. Don't walk at an unrealistic pace, because you will just become exhausted and discouraged, and you'll increase your risk of injury. For now, your goal in walking should be to walk as far as you can for as long as you can. Don't worry about speed. Because of the way your body stores and uses "fuel," you'll be able to burn more calories by keeping to a moderate pace, exercising for a longer time, and covering more distance.

This may contradict your picture of the sweaty, exhausted exerciser, but it has to do with the way the body uses its fuel. The body stores fuel in the forms of carbohydrate and fat. At rest, most of the body's energy comes from carbohydrates stored as glycogen in the liver and muscles. It takes several minutes of aerobic exercise (exercise that forces the heart and lungs to work harder to meet the muscles' demand for oxygen) to get fat out of storage so it can be burned. So in short bursts of effort, such as sprinting, practically all our energy comes from glycogen. But for longer aerobic exercise, such as a half hour of walking, jogging, or swimming, about half our energy comes from glycogen and half from fat. During really prolonged activity—walking, say, for an hour— there will be a significant increase in the amount of fat used. And if you exercise even longer than that, fat will supply almost 90 percent of the needed energy. So the longer you go, the more fat you burn. Fortunately, walking doesn't exhaust you the way jogging can. By walking, you can exercise for a much longer time, even covering more distance, than you can by jogging. This extra time and distance means that you continue to burn extra calories—and more of these extra calories come from fat.

Walking's weight-loss potential is just as flexible as you are. So as your fitness level increases, you can increase the intensity of your walking and the number of calories you burn. By walking at a brisk pace of four or five miles per hour and vigorously pumping your arms, by adding hand-held or round-the-wrist weights (see Chapter 7), or by hiking with a backpack (see Chapter 8), you can increase your calorie burn per hour to nearly the same as with slow to moderate jogging.

Indeed, racewalking (see Chapter 6) can actually burn more calories than jogging at the same pace. At high racewalking speeds (like six or seven miles an hour), your body yearns to break into a jog; forcing yourself to continue walking super-fast—keeping at least one foot on the ground at all times—takes more energy than jogging at the same speed.

There are also substantial slimming payoffs for tackling hilly terrain. Even at a slow pace, going uphill dramatically raises walking's calorie costs, compared with following the same pace on level ground. Surprisingly, even going downhill burns more calories than covering level ground, because it takes extra energy for the body to resist its natural tendency to zoom down the hill too fast. Walking on shifting sand or dirt, rather than rigid asphalt or concrete, can boost the calorie cost by as much as one third.

The advantages of diet-walking don't stop there, either. They may extend long beyond the last step of your daily constitutional. The warm glow you feel after exercising is a sign that your metabolism is still revved up. This quickened metabolic rate can help you burn extra calories after exercise—even while you're resting.

To gauge the success of a diet-walking program, or even to get a handle on your status before you start, the bathroom scale may not tell the whole story. The reason is that fat, rather than weight per se, is what you really want to lose. Fat is less dense than muscle and it weighs less per unit volume, so it's actually possible to be overfat (with too high a proportion of body fat) without being overweight. Conversely, a muscle-bound athlete who is fit and trim and has a very low percentage of body fat may weigh more than weight tables say is desirable because of all of his or her muscle. The range considered healthy for a mature male is 10 to 15 percent of body weight as fat; for a mature woman, 20 to 25 percent.

Some weight-loss centers, clinics, and fitness clubs now offer high-tech measurements of body fat, including underwater weighing (based on the principle that fat is more buoyant than lean tissue) and electrical impedance (based on the principle that fat contains much less water than lean tissue, and water conducts electricity). But body-fat testing need not be this expensive or precise. An older, less precise method is using skin-fold calipers (fat pinchers). You can also get a pretty good idea of your progress in the war against fat by merely looking in the mirror—and trying on your clothes. This makes more sense than weighing yourself too often (once a week is plenty) or getting too obsessed with what the scale has to tell you.

Toning Muscles and Building Strength

You may have noticed that serious walkers have particularly shapely legs—not "toothpick" legs or "thunder thighs." The reason is that walking builds, shapes, and tones muscles all over the legs, hips, and buttocks. Walking also boosts the strength and endurance of those muscles, which means you'll be able to do more without getting as tired.

According to David Winter, Ph.D., professor of kinesiology at the University of Waterloo in Waterloo, Ontario, Canada, these are the main muscle groups affected:

▶ *Calf muscles*—For developing shapely calf muscles, nothing comes close to walking. Walking involves a higher proportion of calf muscle power than does running. The calf muscles provide the upward and forward momentum for the "pushoff" phase of walking, which lifts the heel off the ground.

▶ *Tibialis anterior muscles*—These muscles, which run along the outside of each shin, are toned as they raise the big toe to flex the foot during walking's "swing" phase and lower it after the heel hits the ground.

▶ *Hamstring muscles*—Walking's pushoff phase tones the hamstring muscles in the back of the thighs.

▶ *Quadriceps muscles*—These muscles at the front of the thighs are toned as each leg is extended.

▶ *Hip flexor muscles*—These muscles are toned as each leg stretches forward in the swing phase of the stride.

▶ *Buttock muscles*—Rocking the hips during brisk walking tones your *gluteus maximus*.

▶ *Abdominal muscles*—Making a point of walking with shoulders erect and buttocks tucked in can strengthen these muscles.

▶ *Arm and shoulder muscles*—These muscles are toned when you pump your arms vigorously, up to chest or shoulder level, while walking (the left arm swings forward naturally as the right leg strides ahead, and vice versa).

Methods abound for enhancing walking's muscle-toning action. You'll increase the involvement of the leg-lifting quadriceps by walking uphill—and even downhill. By lengthening your stride and walking faster, you'll demand more of the hamstrings, hip flexors, and buttocks. And by carrying hand-held weights, you'll help tone the arm and shoulder muscles.

To substantially increase strength and muscle tone in the upper body, however, you'll probably need to do ex-

Major Muscles Used in Walking

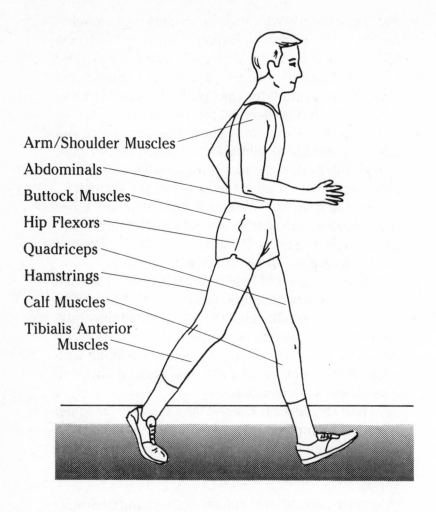

Arm/Shoulder Muscles

Abdominals

Buttock Muscles

Hip Flexors

Quadriceps

Hamstrings

Calf Muscles

Tibialis Anterior Muscles

tra exercises, like push-ups and chin-ups, that concentrate specifically on this area. Weight training is also a good way to augment the strength and endurance effects of walking.

Throughout your walking program, it's very important to stretch your muscles both before and after your walks to maintain your flexibility and ward off injury. In Chapter 9 you'll find a variety of these stretches to choose from and tips on incorporating them in your walking routine.

Building Aerobic Capacity

Like jogging, bicycling, swimming, skating, and cross-country skiing, walking is what is known as an aerobic exercise. That means it is a sustained, repeated, rhythmic workout for large muscle groups. This type of workout requires oxygen and depends on the cardiovascular system (including the heart and blood vessels) to supply this oxygen to the muscles while they work. In contrast, in so-called anaerobic exercises, such as weight lifting or sprinting, the muscles are involved in short bursts of highly intense activity, and they can obtain energy through a chemical process that does not involve oxygen.

Walking at a brisk enough pace offers benefits in the aerobic conditioning component of fitness by "training" your heart, lungs, and skeletal muscles. Like all muscles, the heart becomes better conditioned the more it is used. By engaging in regular aerobic exercise, you improve your heart's ability to pump oxygen-rich blood to your muscles. You also make your muscles more efficient at using oxygen, so they can do more work without putting as great a strain on your heart. By increasing your aerobic capacity, you make more oxygen available to your body. With this increase, you'll be able to exercise longer and harder with less fatigue, and you'll have a slower resting heart rate.

Michael Pollock, Ph.D., director of the University of Florida's Center for Exercise Science, pioneered research into walking's effects on aerobic capacity. He found that walking, jogging, and bicycling all boosted aerobic capacity to the same extent—provided they were done at the same intensity. (As usual, the walking group sustained the fewest injuries and had the lowest dropout rate.)

"However," he cautions, "this improvement in aerobic capacity through walking depends on how hard you do it and for how long." It is possible to walk at such a high speed that you equal the aerobic conditioning benefits of jogging. But at usual walking speeds, walking is less intense than jogging, so you've got to walk longer—or uphill—to get the same training effect as you would get by jogging. Another alternative is to use weights—hand-held weights or a backpack—to increase walking's training effects.

For effective aerobic conditioning, you need to walk for a minimum of 30 minutes at least 3 times a week. And during each walk, you need to work hard enough to get your heart rate into your "target range"—pumping at 60 to 80 percent of its predicted maximum. (See Chapter 4 to learn more about your "target heart range.")

There's a catch to increasing your aerobic capacity, though. The higher your fitness level, the faster you must walk to get fitter. This means walking briskly—at least three miles an hour, for most people, and four for those in better shape.

It's long been assumed that people who have already worked themselves from low or average fitness into top condition can't get any fitness training benefits from walking. But Dr. Pollock says this isn't necessarily so. He found that when fit people walked briskly for 40 minutes, four days a week, they could reach a heart-rate range of 70 to 75 percent of their maximum heart rate reserve—close to the results seen with jogging. The difference: If you walk, you need to increase the frequency and duration of exercise to get the same aerobic conditioning results as jogging.

James Rippe, M.D., director of the Center for Health, Fitness and Human Performance at the University of Massachusetts Medical School in Worcester, has made similar findings. Based on his studies of hundreds of walkers, he says even the fittest can raise their heart rates to 70 to 85 percent of maximum, just by walking. But they have to walk fast—as much as six miles per hour—or uphill.

When aerobic conditioning is achieved, it can have important long-term benefits, including protection against coronary heart disease and stroke. In a study of 3,000 men, conducted at Duke University, the least fit men had about three-and-a-half times the risk of sustaining a fatal heart attack or stroke as did the most fit group during the follow-up period of eight-and-a-half years.

There is a limit to how much exercise can improve one's aerobic capacity, though, says Ronald LaPorte, Ph.D., associate professor of epidemiology at the University of Pittsburgh. An exercise program can increase a person's aerobic capacity by 30 percent at most. The remaining 70 percent of the aerobic capacity is dictated not by your activity level but by your genes—for such things as lung structure and heart size, which determine how much oxygen you breathe, and for body size. Because of these variables, the aerobic capacity of 2 different people may differ by as much as 200 percent.

Walking Through Pregnancy

Doctors often recommend walking as the safest form of aerobic exercise for pregnant women. Women who are habitual walkers are urged to continue walking during their pregnancy, although they may eventually have to slow down a bit because of the extra weight they'll be carrying toward the end of the pregnancy.

Those who have been sedentary are advised to start walking—but gradually, with a very easy, slow start. And those who are accustomed to running may be advised to switch to walking during their pregnancy, to avoid excessive fatigue, breathlessness, and stress on the bones and joints from all the extra weight. Hormonal changes in pregnancy tend to loosen ligaments all over the body in preparation for childbirth, so the joints become more susceptible to injury, especially if subjected to bouncing forces, as in running, or jerky movements, as in tennis. But these jarring forces and movements do not occur in walking, because it is such a low-impact activity.

Even though weight reduction is not allowed during pregnancy, walking can help to control excessive weight gain. Walking can also help guard against the development of varicose veins and edema (swelling in the legs and ankles), to which pregnant women are prone, by increasing circulation and helping to contract the leg veins. And walking may help alleviate the sway-backed posture (called lordosis) that pregnant women may develop.

In the last few years, more attention has been paid to the idea of enlisting the help of gravity in childbirth. When the laboring mother is upright, instead of lying down, gravity can help pull the baby down, putting more pressure on the cervix and, it is thought, speeding up labor. As a consequence, devices such as birthing chairs are gaining favor. And it is also more common for obstetricians and midwives to urge laboring women to change their position frequently, to stand, to squat, and even to walk around during the first stage of labor if they feel like it. This gentle physical exertion can help the time pass for the laboring woman. It can also accelerate labor, and, unlike medications, is devoid of unwanted side effects.

After delivery, a new mother can resume her walking routine within a few days. Special packs are available for carrying infants on the chest while walking (see Chapter 15 for more on these).

Walking Around Injury

One of the biggest problems with strenuous, fitness-boosting exercise is the risk of injury. Although the injury itself may heal in a fairly short time, the damage it does to your motivation and enthusiasm can be long-lasting. Fortunately, a walking program can help you increase your fitness with a relatively small risk of injury.

Injuries to the joints are rare with walking, although not unheard of (see Chapter 10). "I suspect we'll start seeing more walking-related injuries in the future, as walking gains popularity as an exercise form," says Peter Cavanagh, Ph.D., director of the Center for Locomotion Studies at Pennsylvania State University. "But never as many as with running or jogging."

By definition, walking means keeping one foot on the ground at all times—and sometimes two. Therefore, compared with jogging, which involves a free-flight phase, walking poses much less danger of falling; and each foot hits the ground with a force of only one-and-a-quarter times the weight of the body, at most, according to Kevin Campbell, Ph.D., a staff scientist at the Cleveland Clinic Foundation. In contrast, each running stride lands with a force of up to four times body weight. (For jumping, as in high-impact aerobics, this force is up to seven times.)

Such high forces on the feet carry even more stress up the body to the ankle, knee, and hip joints. When internal pressure on the hip joints was measured using an artificial hip implant, the stress associated with jogging was one-and-a-half times greater than that found with walking. And this stress helps explain why so many runners and high-impact aerobic dancers suffer injuries of these joints. People who suffer these injuries often have no choice but to drop out of their joint-jarring exercise programs. In contrast, the lack of these injuries is considered one main reason why walkers stick with their programs.

In a recent study, Dr. Pollock found that 22 people aged 70 were able to work up, gradually, to a program of brisk walking, with no adverse consequences to either their hearts or their joints. However, when 18 of the subjects then graduated to a program of jogging and jog/walking, 60 percent of them suffered significant injuries. "It was not a cardiovascular limitation, but an orthopedic problem," he stresses.

An earlier, related study by Dr. Pollock showed better compliance and fewer injuries with a more moderate exercise program. He compared brief, intense sprinting with mild, continuous jogging, and found that the rates of both injuries and dropouts were double for the more demanding sprinting program—even though the fitness benefits associated with the two activities were essentially identical.

A regular walking program may even help older adults avoid injury by keeping them on their feet. For older adults, particularly those over 70 years old, the incidence of injury linked to falls is higher than for any other group. The neuromuscular changes that occur in aging tend to disturb the sense of balance, which in turn raises the risk of falling and of injury. (Other factors, including medication and osteoporosis, which is discussed in Chapter 2, also play a role in the high incidence of injury.) However, in a recent study, participation in a walking program was shown to improve balance, thereby reducing the risk of falling among older adults. The study compared two groups of older adults: One group participated in the walking program, which involved walking for half an hour, three times a week, for six weeks; the other group maintained their usual low level of activity. Balance was gauged by how long a person could maintain each of these stances: standing on the toes, standing on one foot, standing on one foot on a high beam, and standing on the toes while on a high beam. Balance improved significantly among the subjects who took part in the walking program, but not among those in the sedentary group.

So whether you're trying an exercise program for the first time or retreating from one where gain meant pain, walking fills the bill. A well-designed walking program can help you achieve the five components of fitness. As already discussed, walking can help improve body composition by increasing your body's ratio of muscle to fat. It can help you boost your endurance and increase the strength of the muscles in your lower body. A walking program that includes plenty of stretching exercises can help you maintain flexibility. And, walking can help you increase your aerobic capacity.

You can enhance these fitness benefits by stepping up to a more vigorous walking program—moving faster, racewalking, adding weights, and walking uphill and downhill. However, as will be discussed in Chapter 2, many of the long-term health benefits of walking are seen even with walking programs that are not intense enough to boost fitness significantly. So fitness isn't everything. All activity counts because it improves overall health—even when it's too low-level to greatly increase fitness.

Chapter 2

FOR THE
HEALTH
OF IT

Lifelong, consistent exercise, including walking, has been linked to a host of health benefits—among them, fighting coronary heart disease, aiding in the treatment of high blood pressure, raising levels of "good" (high-density lipoprotein) cholesterol, strengthening bones, helping digestion, and possibly even combating cancer. Walking can also play a role in the treatment of coronary heart disease, respiratory disease, diabetes, and arthritis. And most impressive of all, an active lifestyle has actually been associated with longer life and slower aging.

Fighting Heart Disease

Despite the obvious benefits of a moderate to vigorous aerobic exercise like brisk walking, many experts stress that fitness training isn't the sole road to health.

What's important is activity of any kind, even slow walking, as long as it's done regularly, for a sufficient length of time, throughout a lifetime.

"That's where walking really shines," says Dr. James Rippe of the University of Massachusetts. "Several studies have shown that people who do strenuous exercise, including running, are subject to a high rate of injuries, and they often drop out. Walking is much more often the kind of activity that a person can adopt as a lifelong, consistent program, and that's what counts most—even more than exercise intensity—in terms of long-term health benefits such as reducing the risk of developing heart disease."

In contrast to completely inactive people, walkers have repeatedly been shown to suffer from less coronary heart disease. This means that even slow-paced walking pays off—for people with heart problems, those who are at risk, and those who aren't at risk and want to stay that way. (Heart patients should see the walking programs designed specifically for them in Chapter 5.)

Remember, all activity counts. For instance, says Dr. Ronald LaPorte, epidemiologist at the University of Pittsburgh, "Mothers with young children are extraordinarily active, keeping up with the kids. This activity usually isn't intense enough to improve their fitness, yet it may well be very beneficial to their health."

By concentrating on the middle ground that includes most of us—between utter "couch potatoes" and Olympic athletes—scientists are finding real benefits to moderate activity. Although such activity, including easy-paced walking, on the job or for fun, may not enhance fitness, it still has been shown to help ward off heart disease, the nation's number-one killer. Indeed, an inactive life-style is now considered an independent risk factor for coronary heart disease.

The link between on-the-job activity and heart protection was first found in a study of British postal workers. Mail carriers—who walked all day—had fewer heart attacks than did post office clerks who spent most of their days in one place. Another study, conducted by Ralph Paffenbarger, M.D., professor of epidemiology at Stanford University, found that California longshoremen who were most active on the job were less likely to die of a heart attack than were coworkers who had sedentary jobs. In both cases, the workers' pace was probably too low to greatly boost their aerobic capacity, yet the protection from heart disease occurred anyway.

Similar results have been obtained from studies of leisure-time exercise, including walking. For instance, leisure-time activity has been shown to protect a large group of Harvard graduates against heart disease—actually prolonging their lives. The habitually energetic alumni have been less likely to have a heart attack, and more apt to survive if they did have one.

The still-ongoing study, led by Dr. Paffenbarger, is called the Harvard Alumni Study. It involves nearly 17,000 male alumni of Harvard College and it has had a 12-year follow-up period so far.

The results have shown that, up to a certain point, the more active the alumni have been on their time off, the more they have been protected. This protection increases as the energy spent on leisure activity rises from less than 500 to 2,000 or more calories a week. But the protection actually starts to decline at very high activity levels, above 3,500 calories a week. Death rates from all causes have been one-quarter to one-third lower among the alumni who have spent 2,000 or more calories a week on leisure activity than among the less active men.

The more they have engaged in leisure-time activities, including walking, stair climbing, and playing various sports, the less chance they have had of dying from diseases of the heart, blood vessels, or respiratory system. And this effect remained even after other risk factors, such as high blood pressure, cigarette smoking, weight gains, and family history of early death, were taken into account. In fact, it appears that physical activity might even help lessen the unhealthy effects of cigarette smoking and high blood pressure.

Another major study, called the Multiple Risk Factor Intervention Trial (MRFIT), has also strengthened the connection between leisure-time physical activity, including walking, and protection against heart disease and death. Arthur S. Leon, M.D., professor of epidemiology at the University of Minnesota School of Public Health in Minneapolis, led the seven-year investigation of over 12,000 middle-aged men. All of the men were at high risk for coronary heart disease, because of high blood pressure, cigarette smoking, and high levels of cholesterol in the blood.

Based on questionnaire results, the researchers figured out how many minutes per day each man spent on leisure-time physical activity, including walking, gardening, yard work, home repairs, dancing, and swimming. The men were categorized as having low, moderate, or high levels of leisure activity. The average minutes spent per day on leisure-time physical activity were 15 for the "low" group, 47 for the "moderate" group, and 134 for the "high" group.

When compared with low leisure activity, moderate activity reduced the rate of fatal heart attacks by one-third, and the rate of total deaths by one-quarter, during the seven-year follow-up period. But exercise's benefits were found to peak at the moderate level, with less "bang" for the exercise "buck" after a certain point. Death rates among men with high activity levels were similar to those for men who engaged in only moderate activity.

Walking's benefits are not limited to protection against coronary heart disease, however. Doctors often "prescribe" walking to patients who have heart disease. Studies have shown that after a heart attack or coronary bypass surgery, people who exercise regularly tend to recover more quickly and completely. And walking is favored over other, more strenuous aerobic exercises, such as running, because it carries much less risk of temporarily overloading the heart and provoking sudden death. But walking is not enough by itself to protect heart patients from having a second heart attack, Dr. Rippe warns. They should also quit smoking, eat a diet low in cholesterol and saturated fat, and get treatment if they have high blood pressure.

Just how does walking lower the risk of coronary heart disease? There are several possibilities, and any or all of them may contribute to the protection offered by walking. As discussed in Chapter 1, a rigorous walking program can strengthen your heart and lungs and make your muscles more efficient at using oxygen, thus allowing you to do more without putting as great a strain on your heart. But walking can also play a role by reducing other risk factors for coronary heart disease. For instance, being obese increases your risk of developing coronary heart disease, but as discussed in Chapter 1, walking can help you lose fat and control your weight. As you'll see in Chapter 3, regular walking may help you reduce or deal more effectively with stress, which can take its toll on your heart. Walking can also help raise blood levels of "good" (high-density lipoprotein) cholesterol, aid in the treatment of high blood pressure, and help control diabetes, thus dampening the effects of these risk factors for coronary heart disease.

Walking and Cholesterol

Exercise has not been consistently shown to lower the *total* levels of artery-clogging cholesterol in the blood. (To do that, you need to eat less saturated fat and cholesterol and fewer calories—or take special medications.) But time and again, studies have shown that exercise does have a beneficial effect on the kinds of cholesterol in the blood. Walking can help you increase your ratio of "good" cholesterol (called high-density lipoprotein or HDL) to "bad" cholesterol (called low-density lipoprotein or LDL).

Both LDL and HDL serve as containers that carry cholesterol around in the bloodstream, but they play markedly different roles. LDL deposits cholesterol just where you don't want it, in the cells that line the arteries, thus causing hardening of the arteries or *atherosclerosis*. When this "hardening" occurs in the coronary arteries, it can block the flow of oxygen-rich blood to the heart, eventually causing chest pain (called *angina pectoris*) or a heart attack. HDL, on the other hand, helps rid the bloodstream of excess cholesterol, taking it to the liver where it can be excreted. So it's best to have as much of your cholesterol in HDL, and as little in LDL, as possible. A high ratio of HDL to LDL cholesterol helps protect against coronary heart disease, even when the total cholesterol level is relatively high.

After reviewing the relevant studies, University of Colorado researchers concluded that exercise, especially when combined with weight loss, can increase your HDL level. And it's the distance covered—not the speed or intensity—that really counts. So walking does as well as jogging, as long as enough ground is covered.

The walking that mail carriers do is adequate for raising the level of HDL cholesterol, according to Dr. La-

Porte. The key, he says, is that although it is low-intensity, it is long-duration exercise. With colleagues at the University of Pittsburgh, Dr. LaPorte found a correlation between the miles the postal workers reported walking per day (an average of five) and the level of HDL cholesterol. And this correlation was not reduced even when factors that can affect cholesterol levels, such as age, alcohol consumption, body mass, and leisure-time activity, were taken into account.

Men and women who are endurance-trained athletes tend to have 30 to 50 percent more HDL cholesterol than do their less-active counterparts, according to William L. Haskell, Ph.D., associate professor of medicine and deputy director of the Center for Research in Disease Prevention at Stanford University School of Medicine. Even people who engage in vigorous on-the-job or recreational activity, including walking, may have about ten percent more HDL cholesterol than those who are sedentary. Some studies have suggested that an activity threshold of as little as ten miles per week may make a difference in HDL levels.

But if you're walking to improve your cholesterol profile, you need to keep a couple of points in mind. For starters, the higher the initial concentration of HDL cholesterol, the harder it is to raise. And exercise programs don't boost HDL cholesterol levels overnight. It takes time—and miles.

Walking and High Blood Pressure

Exercise, including walking, may help people with high blood pressure to keep their disease under control. And that's good news, because high blood pressure raises the risks of coronary heart disease, stroke, and kidney disease.

Scientific research has not consistently shown that exercise lowers blood pressure. Yet there seems to be enough evidence to convince doctors to include a regular exercise program in the treatment of this disease. In a recent Australian study, conducted at the Baker Medical Research Institute in Melbourne, moderate regular exercise reduced mild high blood pressure to almost the same levels that could be achieved with antihypertensive medications. In general, however, studies seem to indicate that while regular exercise doesn't normalize blood pressure, it may lower it by about ten millimeters of mercury, abbreviated *mmHG*. (When blood pressure is measured, the gauge shows pressure by indicating the level of mercury in a glass tube.)

In addition, by aiding in long-term weight loss and control, and thus warding off obesity, walking may indirectly lower blood pressure. Overweight is a risk factor for high blood pressure, and losing weight tends to lower blood pressure.

In people whose blood pressure is well within normal limits, studies have not shown that exercise lowers blood pressure. It is thought, however, that regular exercise may help prevent the development of high blood pressure.

Unlike aerobic capacity, which keeps improving with more and more strenuous exercise, blood pressure may do best with mild to moderate exercise, according to Edward Zambrowsky, Ph.D., an associate professor of physiology at Rutgers University. In laboratory animals bred for high blood pressure, exercise's ability to lower blood pressure was most pronounced at moderate, or relatively low, intensity—not at high intensity.

"How the exercise is perceived may also be important," says Dr. Zambrowsky. "Voluntary exercise appears to lower blood pressure more than forced exercise does."

For instance, when people with high blood pressure were encouraged to exercise voluntarily, following their own whims, their blood pressure decreased more than if they were forced to follow a prescribed exercise program. Similar results have been found in lab animals. It is possible that forced, high-intensity exercise is perceived as a stress, which counteracts any lowering of blood pressure. In contrast, a life peppered with walks, done without any coercion, may lower stress reactions and protect against high blood pressure.

Research by exercise physiologist Michael Pollock and his colleagues has indicated that blood pressure can actually *increase* significantly during walking with hand-held weights. Thus, some people whose blood pressure is already high might want to avoid holding weights in their hands while walking. But it doesn't mean giving up weights entirely. "We discovered that hand gripping is what makes the blood pressure rise," he says. "So we teach people to relax their hands as much as possible, or have them wrap the weights around their wrists, and they don't get that increase in blood pressure." (See Chapter 7 for more on walking with weights.)

Exercising for Diabetes

A regular walking program can be one of the keys to controlling mild, "adult-onset" diabetes. As its name implies, this type of diabetes usually doesn't develop until middle age, and it can often be controlled without taking insulin or any other medications.

Walking can play an indirect, but important role in this type of diabetes by aiding in weight loss. About 80 percent of people with adult-onset diabetes are overweight. But by losing weight and keeping it off they can control their disease much more easily.

A regular walking program can also help people with adult-onset diabetes to control their blood sugar levels. Exercise helps stem the abnormal rise in blood sugar that occurs after diabetics consume carbohydrates. It can also increase sensitivity to insulin—a chemical, normally produced by the body, that moves sugar into the cells.

The benefits of walking are not as clear cut when it comes to the other major form of the disease, called "juvenile-onset" or "insulin-dependent" diabetes. Although diet and exercise may play important roles in managing this form of diabetes, insulin is required to get it under control. Some studies have suggested that exercise can help decrease blood sugar levels and insulin needs in juvenile-onset diabetes; but as yet the case isn't considered as strong as for the adult-onset form.

Diabetics who want to exercise, however, need to be cautious. Because they are at a higher risk of developing coronary heart disease, they should consult their doctors and have a stress test done before starting any exercise program. They also need to take special care of their feet. People with diabetes who develop nerve damage (neuropathy) are in danger of sustaining an injury without feeling it, and thus letting it worsen. And because their circulation tends to be poor, particularly in the feet, it is harder for them to fight off foot infections. Even blisters can "snowball" into infected skin ulcers. So, diabetics who want to exercise regularly should do so only under the guidance of a doctor.

Helping in Respiratory Disease

With mild exercise such as walking, people with asthma or chronic lung disease can improve the condition of their respiratory muscles and the efficiency of their skeletal muscles. As the skeletal muscles become more efficient, they require less oxygen to do the same amount of work.

But people with exercise-induced asthma should take special precautions, such as taking their medications just before exerting themselves, especially if they plan to work out in cold, dry air. If you have a respiratory disease, be sure to check with your doctor before beginning an exercise program.

Warding Off Osteoporosis

In terms of exercise's long-term benefits, there may be such a thing as exercising too much. For example, excessive running can actually raise a woman's risk of developing the bone-thinning disease called osteoporosis, which can cause pain, broken bones, stooped posture, and loss of height. This happens when exercise is performed so strenuously and so often that it causes extreme leanness. (Excessive dieting can also cause extreme leanness.) At only about ten pounds under her ideal body weight, a woman may lack sufficient fat to produce very much of the sex hormone estrogen or to have regular menstrual periods. Estrogen helps keep the bones strong and protects against osteoporosis. So by sapping the body's estrogen supply, excessive exercise may set the stage for osteoporosis, even at a young age.

Performed in moderation, however, activity can help ward off osteoporosis. Exercises such as walking, running, and racket sports, in which the body bears its own weight, have been shown to strengthen the muscles and bones and protect against problems in later life, including osteoporosis. This happens because weight-bearing exercise increases bone density. With the aid of gravity, muscles pull on bones, and they stimulate the bone to take up more of the bone-strengthening mineral calcium.

On the other hand, with prolonged inactivity—for instance, when a broken limb is placed in a cast—the muscles and bones can start to waste away (atrophy). Even astronauts who experience weightlessness from living in atmospheres without gravity begin to lose bone mass.

A study conducted at the University of Pittsburgh indicated that walking can slow down bone thinning, not only in the leg bones but all over the body. In the study, over 250 postmenopausal women were divided into 2 groups: One group started a walking program and the other stayed sedentary. After three years, bone thinning was significantly slowed in the arm bones of the walking women when compared with those of the sedentary women.

Protection against osteoporosis is an important health benefit, because this disease leaves so many women vulnerable to fractures of the spine, hips, and wrists when their natural estrogen levels plummet after menopause. Consequently, a National Institutes of Health consensus panel has recommended a program of modest weight-bearing exercise to help prevent osteoporosis. And as discussed in Chapter 1, walking may also benefit women who have osteoporosis by improving their balance and thus decreasing their risk of falling and injuring their fragile bones.

Walking for Arthritis

Arthritis can make the first step too painful to think about, and doctors once advised their arthritic patients against exercise. But walking is now being used more and more in the management of arthritis, according to the American Arthritis Association. Persevering and gradually putting one foot in front of the other, going a bit farther each day, often pays off for arthritis patients. A regular walking program can help fight the pain and stiffness of arthritis, as well as build strength to enable arthritis sufferers to carry out the activities of daily life and maintain their independence.

The association recommends starting with a short walk that doesn't cause any more pain than when you started. Then gradually increase the distance you cover, with an eventual goal of walking one mile, four times a week. Like others with special health problems, people with arthritis should consult a doctor before starting a walking program (see Chapter 4).

Aiding Digestion

Regular exercise, including walking, can help keep the bowels regular and prevent constipation. It works in much the same way that a fiber-rich diet does, speeding up sluggish digestion. So before you start swigging down over-the-counter preparations for constipation, try going for a brisk walk.

Combating Cancer

Exercise has been associated with lower risks of certain types of cancer, although the link is not as strong as it is in warding off heart disease or osteoporosis. For instance, in Dr. Paffenbarger's study of Harvard alumni, exercise lowered death rates not only from heart disease but also from a variety of types of cancer.

In another ongoing study, led by Harvard's Dr. Rose Frisch, women who started athletic training in their youth adopted life-styles that lowered their risks of developing cancer of the breast and of the reproductive organs. The study involves over 5,000 women who graduated from 10 American colleges since 1925. Three-quarters of the women who were athletic in college have continued active life-styles, but only half of their less active classmates have taken up the exercise habit since their inactive college years. Compared with the college athletes, the less active classmates have had almost twice the incidence of breast cancer and about two and a half times the incidence of cancer of the uterus, ovary, cervix, and vagina. Grouped together, these cancer types make up more than 40 percent of all cancers in women.

The active women in this study are mostly joggers, doing regular, moderately intense exercise. They're not marathon runners, but they *are* active enough to be significantly leaner, and to produce less estrogen than do those in the less active control group. At this point, it is not clear what level of physical activity is necessary to get the anti-cancer effect.

Also unclear is whether any factors other than exercise itself have contributed to the lower cancer risk. For instance, the less active women produce more estrogen, which has been proposed as a risk factor for cancers of the reproductive system. The more active women in the study tend to be leaner and to make healthier food choices than do the less active women—with fewer calories and less saturated fat. Some studies have linked saturated fat intake and obesity with a higher risk of breast cancer, so the active group's food choices and leanness may help explain at least some of exercise's apparent anti-cancer effect.

Exercise also appears to influence the occurrence of colon cancer. The risk of developing cancer of the colon was found to be one-third higher for men in sedentary occupations than for those in active jobs, in a recently concluded study that followed 1.1 million Swedish men for 19 years. In an earlier study, conducted at the University of Southern California, the colon cancer risk was 60 percent higher in men with sedentary occupations than in men with more active jobs. Men whose jobs were considered sedentary included accountants, bookkeepers, lawyers, and musicians; those deemed active included carpenters, gardeners, mail carriers, and plumbers. And in a study done at the State University of New York at Buffalo, the risk of colon cancer was double for people who spent more than 40 percent of their work years in sedentary jobs than for those who had always worked at active jobs.

The effect of exercise on the risk of colon cancer may have something to do with digestion and bowel habits. By speeding up digestion, exercise may shorten the time that the colon (and the rest of the digestive tract) comes in contact with any cancer-causing materials that are being excreted.

Slowing Down Aging

It can be depressing to think about the physical changes we consider to be a natural part of aging—including wasting away of muscle and bone, joint stiffening, and the tendency to get out of breath after only minor exertion. But it's possible that many of these changes are related more to inactivity, which older people too often fall into, than age per se. Many of these changes can occur at any age with extreme inactivity. You've probably experienced this for yourself if you've ever had an extended illness that forced you to stay in bed for a prolonged period of time. When you could finally get out of bed, you probably felt stiff, weak, and "old." So even at a young age, these changes are prevented only by activity. Conversely, although some of these changes may be—to a certain extent—inevitable, older people who remain active often appear (and feel) considerably younger than their years.

Beyond these impressions linking activity with slower aging, hard facts are now becoming available. A study by Dr. Pollock has shown that a program of regular exercise helps delay and even stop the decline in the aerobic capacity of older athletes, actually maintaining their bodies' ability to deliver oxygen to working muscles. Other studies have shown that aerobic capacity is higher in active older people than in inactive ones, even though aerobic capacity generally declines with age. Also, as mentioned earlier in this chapter, a program of weight-bearing exercise like walking can help strengthen bones and prevent that fragile, stooped look so often associated with advanced age.

In Dr. Leon's study of data from the Multiple Risk Factor Intervention Trial, moderate activity resulted in a lower rate of deaths from all causes, not just from heart disease, in middle-aged men at high heart risk. And in Dr. Paffenbarger's study of Harvard alumni, the activity-associated decline in risk of death from diseases of the heart, blood vessels, and respiratory system translates into longer life. "By the age of 80, the amount of additional life attributable to adequate exercise, as compared with sedentariness, was 1 to more than 2 years," according to Dr. Paffenbarger.

Many a comedian has quipped that it is hardly worth the trouble to gain an extra two years of life from jogging, if that means spending all of the added time sweating and struggling down a running track. But regular walking can do more than add a couple of years to your life. With all its health benefits, walking can make your later years more enjoyable—freeing you from unnecessary pain and debility. Indeed, it has often been said that not only can walking add years to your life, it can add life to your years. As you will see in Chapter 3, walking can do more than keep you in shape and protect you from osteoporosis and coronary heart disease. It can help you fight depression and anxiety and perhaps even improve your outlook on life. Besides, walking is widely considered more fun than jogging—feeling good while you do it, not just when you stop. By filling your life with pleasurable walks, you could end up having the last laugh.

Chapter 3

LEAVE THE BLAHS BEHIND

Physical fitness and increased health are not the only payoffs of starting and maintaining a lifelong fitness walking program. Various types of aerobic exercise, including walking, have also been found to help promote mental health—boosting energy, improving sleep, relieving tension and stress, and combating anxiety and depression. Mastering a walking program can give you the true sense of accomplishment that comes from doing something good for your body. In fact, one great reason to walk is that it makes you feel better all around.

A few years ago, the National Institute of Mental Health (NIMH) convened a panel to examine the effects of exercise on mental health. The panel noted a real, proven link between physical fitness and mental health and well-being. Exercise was deemed generally beneficial for the emotional health of people of all ages and both sexes.

Boosting Energy

Many people suffer from a type of chronic fatigue that isn't caused by illness or disease. They endure the blahs during the day and then toss and turn at night— only to wake up the next morning feeling groggy and drained. They might be surprised to learn, however, that a great way to increase their daytime energy levels is to expend energy on regular exercise like walking.

In a recent study conducted at the Institute for Aerobics Research in Dallas, aerobic exercises, including fast walking, were found to combat chronic fatigue in 400 men and women who were initially out of shape but who boosted their physical fitness over a two-and-a-half year period. The researchers favor the following scenario to explain this energy rise: Through routine aerobic exercise, the people increased their physical fitness, which improved their self-esteem. In other words, they felt better about themselves and developed a more optimistic, energetic frame of mind. In addition, the exercisers enhanced the strength and endurance of their muscles and developed the ability to move more efficiently, thus making their daily activities easier to perform—and to face.

Other studies have also supported a link between aerobic exercise, enhanced physical stamina, and a more energetic frame of mind. Walking can help relieve anxiety and boredom. And walking-linked energy boosts can even show up in improved concentration and better performance in mental work on the job or at school.

Several explanations have been proposed for the association between aerobic exercise and increased alertness. For instance, exercise may act by improving circulation and increasing the availability of oxygen to the brain. Increased alertness may also be a side benefit of the raised metabolic rate that occurs during—and for some time after—an exercise bout. In addition, exercise causes the body to produce several chemicals, including adrenaline, which promote mental alertness.

Improving Sleep

Walking can also boost your daytime energy levels by helping you sleep longer and sounder at night. When the President's Council on Physical Fitness asked seven medical experts to rate the sleep-promoting abilities of a whole gamut of physical activities, walking was among the best. Walking beat out many popular sports, such as handball, squash, basketball, calisthenics, tennis, downhill skiing, softball, golf, and bowling. The only activities that garnered better ratings than walking were jogging, swimming, bicycling, skating, and cross-country skiing.

Some people do find, however, that performing intense exercise just before bedtime revs them up so much that they have difficulty falling asleep. So if you intend to walk at a brisk pace, you may need to schedule your walks for at least an hour before you plan to hit the sack. On the other hand, an easy-paced, late night stroll may be just the thing to relax your body and clear your mind so you can fall asleep.

Relieving Stress

You're at work. Your boss calls. You have to hand in that big report two weeks early. Your blood pressure surges. Your pulse races. You start seeing red. What are you going to do?

Before you blow up and give the boss a piece of your mind, try going for a stress-busting, lunch-hour walk. Taking time out to pursue an activity like walking can get your mind off distressing concerns and give you a feeling of detachment from daily pressures. By relaxing and giving your mind the room to wander, you may be able to see the situation in a new light. You may even come up with a solution to your problem.

Stress can be thought of as the need to adapt to a change. But stress is not always negative. With strong coping strategies, you can handle stress and use it creatively as a call to positive action. Stress-related problems arise when you cannot figure out how to adapt to a stressful change. Instead, you find yourself mentally spinning your wheels like a hamster in a cage.

When you feel threatened by a stressful situation, your body automatically prepares you for action. It produces hormones that quicken your pulse, tense your muscles, raise your blood pressure, and sharpen your senses. This "fight or flight" mechanism was a life-saver in earlier times when humans had to cope with physical danger every day. Even today it comes in handy when you're forced into a situation that requires quick *action*. Unfortunately, most of the stressful situations you're faced with in modern life probably don't require a physical fight or flight. Instead, all this physiological commotion builds up—putting you on edge and keeping you there. Unless you find a way of coping with the situation and relieving the pent-up energy, you leave yourself open to a variety of stress-related psychiatric symptoms, like anxiety and aggression, not to mention physical ailments such as high blood pressure, tension headaches, and digestive disorders.

At some time, we all need a way out of this wheel-spinning stress trap. We need a constructive method of releasing physical energy and emotional stress. Exercise can provide that safety valve. In particular, walking can help relieve stress, thus improving your mood and mental outlook.

The NIMH panel on exercise and mental health concluded that exercise lowers a variety of signs of stress, including tension in the nerves and muscles, resting heart rate, and levels of some hormones that serve as messengers of stress. Exercise may also reduce stress emotions, including anxiety, anger, aggression, and tension.

In a study conducted at the University of Kansas, people who were physically fit were better able to cope with stressful life changes such as divorce, death of a loved one, and switching jobs in the previous year. Responding to these stressful changes, they complained of fewer health problems and symptoms of depression than did the people in the study who were less physically fit.

A later study showed that the heart rates of people who had participated in a 13-week aerobic training program increased much less in response to an experimentally induced mental stress than did the heart rates of their sedentary counterparts. The stress involved reading six series of five numbers each, and then repeating them backward from memory. One possible explanation of this result is that mastering any skill, including a successful walking program, may boost self-confidence and coping abilities.

There are several stress-busting approaches to walking. It can be regarded as a social activity, offering an opportunity to share the joy of doing something with friends or family. Conversely, it can also be done alone, with the freedom to think solitary thoughts and compete with no one but yourself.

Walking is also one of the most relaxing workouts. The process of walking comes as naturally as breathing, so one advantage over other activities is that there is no need to concentrate on physical technique. With the body on "automatic pilot," the mind is free to wander during the walk.

On the other hand, when stressed-out people are plagued by negative, unproductive thoughts during their walks, they can crowd out those thoughts by concentrating on their walking technique or their breathing. For instance, when you combine walking with taking long, deep breaths, your mind tends to become more aware and alert. After narrowing your thoughts down to walking or breathing, you can then choose to invite into your conscious mind only those thoughts that are positive and uplifting. In this way, you can change your whole outlook—easing the way for confidence and peace of mind to replace stress, fear, and depression.

To help relieve the myriad aches and pains associated with stress, such as stiff shoulders and cricks in the neck, special massages and exercises are useful additions to a walking program. Tension-relaxing massage should involve firm but gentle circular strokes, with extra attention to knots and tender spots, especially in the stress-storing shoulders and neck. Stretching exercises such as neck rolls and shoulder shrugs can help loosen tight muscles.

Walkers can even concentrate on relaxing their muscles *as* they walk. To do this, simply focus on a particular muscle or muscle group—such as your shoulder, neck, or jaw muscles. Tense the muscles for a few steps as you walk, then slowly release the tension. As you do this, pay attention—feel the tightness slipping away. Then do the same for another muscle until you've tensed and relaxed muscles from your forehead down to your toes. (Be sure to watch for cars, traffic lights, and potholes, though.)

Combating Depression

Clinical depression is defined as sadness that is greater and more prolonged than is warranted by any objective reason. It is characterized by withdrawal, inactivity, dullness, and feelings of helplessness and loss of control. For many people with clinical depression, regular exercise (three times a week or more appears to work best) has been shown to act as a mood elevator.

Doctors, it seems, are convinced by the evidence in favor of using exercise to treat depression. In a recent survey of 1,750 doctors, 85 percent reported that they prescribed exercise—including walking—for treating depression (and 60 percent prescribed exercise to treat anxiety).

The NIMH panel on exercise's effects on mental health concluded that long-term exercise reduces depression in people who start out moderately depressed. In those who are severely depressed, exercise appears to be a useful addition to professional treatment, including medication, electroshock treatment, and psychotherapy. (Combining exercise with antidepressant medication demands close medical supervision.)

In a University of Wisconsin study, exercise even appeared to be as effective as psychotherapy at relieving moderate depression. People with moderate depression were randomly assigned to either psychotherapy or exercise programs. After a year, over 90 percent of the people who had been assigned to the exercise program were no longer depressed. Half of the patients in the psychotherapy group, however, had come back for more treatment.

In people who are not depressed, exercise may enhance self-esteem. However, the NIMH panel noted, studies of nondepressed people have failed to link exercise (especially heavy exercise) to statistically significant improvements in mood. But many people who are not depressed do insist that exercise makes them feel happier. So it is possible that these studies just have not measured the right factors, according to one panel member. Why is walking helpful in the treatment—and perhaps even the prevention—of depression? Following any exercise program, including walking, gives participants a sense of self-reliance, self-mastery, power, and control, because they are getting out and doing something for and by themselves, says Robert S. Brown, M.D., Ph.D., clinical associate professor of behavioral medicine and psychiatry at the University of Virginia in Charlottesville.

Exercise gives people a real opportunity to set and achieve goals and to see and measure personal improvement. This can be very gratifying. One way to enhance this effect and visualize walking accomplishments is to use a daily log or journal. By writing down the speed of each walk and the distance covered, the walker can keep track of improvement. (See Chapter 13 for more information on recording walking progress.)

Particularly to a person who has been sedentary, depressed, or both, and who is plagued by feelings of worthlessness and incompetence, even moderate exercise accomplishments can provide a feeling approaching heroism. It may be necessary, however, for depressed people to fight their unfortunate tendency to push themselves too far, to be too self-critical, and to set impossibly high goals for themselves. By sticking to one of the programs in this book and gradually increasing the intensity of their workouts, they may be able to fight this urge to push too far, too quickly.

Walking may also promote feelings of pleasure, tranquility, and well-being and help relieve pain by encouraging the production of the body's natural opiates, called *endorphins*. These chemical cousins of morphine are responsible for the familiar feeling of euphoria called the "runner's high," and may produce a milder form of this feeling during walking.

Another possible explanation is that exercise like walking can help distract depressed people from their feelings of sadness. Simply going through the motions of confident striding may be enough to build a walker's confidence—like an actor getting in character by donning the appropriate costume and makeup. Also, since regular aerobic exercise is an important aid in losing weight and toning muscles, exercisers may feel the general sense of well-being that stems from knowing they look and feel better.

The very simplest explanation may be that walking just plain feels good. And unlike some more strenuous exercises, it feels good while you're doing it, not just when you stop.

Chapter 4

GETTING READY TO GO

Before you embark on the freestyle walking program that we've developed, you need to consider a few preliminaries, including your overall health, your age, and your eating habits. You also need to learn how to measure your heart rate and listen to your body, so you'll know where to begin and how hard you need to work to increase your fitness and health.

Checking Up On Your Health

Do you have any questions about your health? Even if the answer is "no," it may be a good idea to consult your doctor and go in for a checkup or physical exam before you hit the trail or treadmill, especially if you've been inactive up to now. If you are overweight, over 45, or have any significant health problems, your doctor's "OK" is essential before you begin any exercise program.

Too many Americans have a tendency to take their health for granted and allow too much time to elapse between physical examinations. Unfortunately, life-threatening diseases like high blood pressure and coronary heart disease may not produce symptoms until a good deal of damage is already done. So in order to check up on your health and avoid problems while you're exercising, you may want to visit your doctor for a physical examination before you begin your walking program. If you smoke, a checkup is definitely a good idea, since smoking is a risk factor for a host of health problems.

The physical examination should include a check of your heart and lungs and measurement of your pulse and blood pressure. It may also include an analysis of your blood cholesterol levels and a resting electrocardiogram, which measures electrical signals from your heart while you are resting.

In some cases, the doctor may decide that you also need an exercise test, which is nothing more than an electrocardiogram that is taken while you are exercising on a treadmill or stationary bicycle. Doctors often recommend an exercise test to people who have a personal or family history of heart disease, since these people may have a higher risk of suffering cardiovascular problems during exercise.

An exercise test is also often recommended for people who are over 45 years old—particularly if they have been very inactive; are obese; smoke cigarettes; have high blood pressure, high blood sugar levels, or a high cholesterol level; or have a family history of heart disease. Even if you're under 45, your doctor may give you an exercise test if you have two or more risk factors associated with coronary heart disease or have a history of chest pain or other symptoms of heart disease.

Health Problems

If you are seriously overweight or have any significant health problems like arthritis, anemia, lower back pain, foot trouble, diabetes, or a disorder of the heart, lungs, kidney, or liver, you're probably already getting regular medical checkups. Even so, you need to consult your doctor before you begin walking to make sure the program is safe for you and to find out if you need to take any special precautions. Your doctor can also help you adjust your walking program to suit your ability and needs.

For instance, if you have asthma, your doctor may advise you of ways to prevent exercise-induced attacks, especially if you plan to walk outside in cold, dry weather. If you are diabetic or obese, your doctor may want you to add nonweight-bearing activities—like swimming and walking in a pool—to your walking program to take a load off your feet. If you have insulin-dependent diabetes, your doctor may advise you of when and where (if injections are needed) to take your insulin.

Aging

Your age, in itself, shouldn't keep you from walking. As discussed in Chapter 2, many of the physiological changes that are assumed to be an inevitable part of aging can actually be linked to inactivity. So regular exercise like walking can actually help you look and feel younger. However, even the most active older people cannot avoid all the changes that occur over time.

For instance, with increasing age, the maximum rate at which the heart can beat declines and the risk of coronary heart disease rises. Particularly in women, the bones thin with age, leaving them more susceptible to injury. This happens, to some extent, no matter how healthy your diet has been or how much weight-bearing exercise you've done; these good practices can slow the bone-thinning process, but they don't prevent it entirely. Time also takes its toll on the joints of the body, with the incidence of arthritis climbing in the later years.

For these reasons, people over the age of 45 should consult a doctor and have a checkup before starting any new exercise program.

Eating Right

To make the most of your health and fitness, you need to do more than exercise regularly. You also need to eat a sensible, well-balanced diet that includes a variety of healthy foods. After all, you can't expect your body to work well if you don't supply it with the nutrients it needs. And you can't expect to greatly improve your health or your figure with poor eating habits. So before you take to the road, take a look at your diet.

The American Heart Association (AHA) recommends following a "prudent" diet that is low in fat and cholesterol and high in complex carbohydrates, such as bread, potatoes, cereals, and pasta. (This diet is generally recommended for people over age two. However, it may be unsuitable for diabetics and people with other specific health problems—so check with your doctor.)

According to the AHA, at least 50 percent of the calories you consume should come from carbohydrates, 15 percent from protein, and a maximum of 30 percent from fat. You need to pay attention to the type of fat you consume, too. No more than 10 percent of your total calories should come from saturated fats, like those in meat, dairy products, and coconut and palm oil; no more than

10 percent should come from polyunsaturated fats, like those in soft margarine, mayonnaise, corn oil, sunflower oil, and safflower oil; and the rest should come from monounsaturated fats, like those in chicken, fish, peanut butter, vegetable shortening, and olive oil. You should also limit your cholesterol intake to less than 300 milligrams (mg) per day.

In contrast, most Americans now eat less carbohydrate and more cholesterol and fat—particularly saturated fat, which has been fingered as a major culprit in coronary heart disease. According to the AHA, the average American consumes about 40 percent of total calories in fat, including 15 to 20 percent of calories as saturated fat; only 40 to 45 percent as carbohydrates; and 15 to 20 percent as protein. The average American also consumes as much as 500 mg of cholesterol a day.

You don't have to starve yourself or give up all of your favorite foods in order to improve your eating habits. Instead, you can make gradual, moderate changes in your diet—such as switching from whole milk to low-fat milk or cutting back on the number of eggs you eat each week—to help lower your risk of coronary heart disease and control your weight.

You also don't have to be a wiz at figures to get a handle on your diet. One easy way to keep track of what you're eating and improve your food choices is to consider your diet as being composed of four food groups: 1) milk and dairy products; 2) meat and other high-protein products like beans and nuts; 3) fruits and vegetables; and 4) cereals and grains. Each day, you should have two or more servings from the first group, two or more from the second, four or more from the third, and four or more from the fourth. The accompanying chart illustrates the food group plan and provides suggestions for choosing the healthiest foods from each group.

THE "BASIC FOUR" FOOD GROUP PLAN
A Recommended Daily Guide

Milk Group
2 or more servings/adults
4 or more servings/teenagers
3 or more servings/children

Choose low-fat (0-1%) milk products that are fortified with vitamins A and D. A serving = 8 oz milk; 8 oz yogurt; 1½ cups cottage cheese; 1 cup milk pudding; 1-2 oz cheese.

Meat Group
2 or more servings

Remove skin from poultry, choose only lean cuts of meat, and limit whole eggs to no more than 2 a week. A serving = 2-3 oz cooked meat, fish, or chicken; 1/4 cup tuna; 2 eggs; 4 tbsps peanut butter; 1 cup cooked dried peas or beans; 1/2 cup nuts.

Fruit/Vegetable Group
4 or more servings

Dark green, leafy, or orange vegetables and fruit recommended several times weekly. Citrus fruit recommended daily.
A serving = 1/2 cup fruit, vegetable, or juice; 1 medium-sized piece of fruit.

Grain Group
4 or more servings

Whole grain and enriched breads and cereals are recommended. A serving = 1 slice bread; 1/2 cup cooked cereal; 1 oz ready-to-eat cereal; 1/2 cup cooked rice, grits, macaroni, or spaghetti.

In addition to the "Basic Four" plan, the following recommendations from the AHA can help you make gradual, healthy changes in your cooking and eating habits:

► Eat a variety of foods from the various food groups to help you get all the nutrients you need and to keep mealtime from becoming a bore.

► Choose lean cuts of meat and trim any visible fat.

► Limit the amount of lean meat, fish, and poultry you eat to no more than six ounces a day.

► Substitute vegetable proteins such as dried beans, peas, or legumes for meat proteins as often as you can.

► Choose fish, poultry, and veal more often than beef, lamb, or pork.

► Trim the skin off of poultry before cooking.

► Substitute skim milk and low-fat cheeses for whole milk products.

► Eat no more than two whole eggs or egg yolks a week. Try substituting two egg whites for one whole egg in recipes.

► Cook with liquid vegetable oils and margarines instead of butter or other solid fats.

► Avoid frying foods. Instead, use cooking methods that help remove fat, such as baking, boiling, broiling, roasting, or stewing.

The prudent diet is a good one, particularly for active people. The active person, including the walker, requires a diet fairly high in complex carbohydrates (from grains, cereals, fruits, and vegetables), to supply the energy necessary for exercising.

You should probably wait at least two hours after your last meal to begin an intense bout of exercise. Otherwise, your digestive tract will be competing with your working muscles for oxygen-carrying blood. Usually, the muscles win out, interfering with digestion, making you feel bloated, and sometimes causing cramps.

The best meal to eat before a long or intense walking workout is one high in complex carbohydrates—rather than fat or protein, which take longer to digest. Sugar (a simple carbohydrate) is no substitute for these complex carbohydrates; nor is it a good idea to eat foods high in sugar shortly before exercising. Despite popular lore, loading up on sugar will not help fuel your activity, because it takes about 20 to 30 minutes for the energy from the sugar to be made available to your muscles. A pre-exercise sugar binge can also cause a surge of insulin, which paradoxically results in low blood sugar during the activity—and that can seriously hinder your performance during a long walk.

Exercise does not significantly raise a person's requirements for protein or for most vitamins and minerals. (Exercise *does* slightly increase the need for the B vitamins, which can be obtained by eating whole-grain or enriched cereals.) So there is no reason for the active person to load up on extra protein servings or to gulp down vitamin or mineral supplements.

It is particularly important for the active person to drink plenty of water. There is no good reason to restrict fluid intake. You should drink water before, during, and after exercise—particularly in warm weather—even if you don't feel particularly thirsty. As a thirst quencher, water is tough to beat.

Following Your Heart

The walking programs in the next chapter will take you step-by-step down the road to increased health and fitness. But since your body is like no one else's, you'll need your own personal guide to tell you where to begin and how much physical effort you need to put in. Your best bet? Follow your heart. Your heart rate can tell you when you're working hard enough to increase your aerobic fitness.

Exercise physiologists have figured out a heart rate range that is safe for most people during exercise. They call this your *target heart rate range.* Your target heart rate range is between 60 percent and 90 percent of your maximum heart rate. (Your maximum heart rate is the number of times your heart beats when you're putting in your maximum effort.)

This range tells you your optimum level of exertion during exercise. That doesn't mean you can't get any health or fitness benefits by exercising below or above that range. Indeed, as discussed in earlier chapters, an activity as mild as gardening may provide some benefit. It's just that keeping your heart rate in the 60 percent to 90 percent range during regular aerobic exercise has been shown to be safe and effective for increasing your aerobic fitness. (Exercising above this range can be very uncomfortable and may increase your risk of injury.) If you've been inactive, however, it's best to start gradually, with a target zone of 50 percent to 60 percent of your maximum heart rate.

To find your target heart rate range, you first need to know your maximum heart rate. An exercise test can tell you your precise maximum heart rate. But if you haven't taken an exercise test, you can get an estimate of your maximum heart rate by subtracting your age from 220. For example, if you are 25 years old, your maximum heart rate is 220 minus 25, or about 195 beats per minute. If you're 48 years old, your maximum heart rate is 220 minus 48, or about 172 beats per minute. This is an approximation. Your actual maximum heart rate can vary by as many as 25 beats per minute. If you are older

YOUR TARGET HEART RATE RANGE

By exercising at 60 percent to 90 percent of your maximum heart rate for at least 20 minutes, three or more days a week, you can safely and effectively increase your aerobic fitness. We recommend that you work up to the target range gradually by following the walking programs outlined in the next chapter. The maximum heart rates shown are estimates obtained by subtracting age from 220. To find your precise maximum heart rate, you need to take an exercise test.

Age	Maximum Heart Rate (Beats per minute)	Target Heart Rate Range (Between 60 percent and 90 percent of maximum in beats per minute)
20	200	120 to 180
25	195	117 to 175
30	190	114 to 171
35	185	111 to 166
40	180	108 to 162
45	175	105 to 157
50	170	102 to 153
55	165	99 to 148
60	160	96 to 144
65	155	93 to 139
70	150	90 to 135

or have heart problems, therefore, it may be a good idea to have an exercise test done to find out your precise maximum.

Once you know your maximum heart rate, you can multiply it by .6 (60 percent) and .9 (90 percent) respectively to find the lower and upper limits of your target heart rate range. For example, if your maximum heart rate is 180 beats per minute, then your target heart rate range is between 108 (180 × .6) and 162 (180 × .9) beats per minute.

To check your heart rate, you need a watch that measures seconds, not just minutes. You can take your pulse either at the radial artery in your wrist (on the inner side of your wrist, below the heel of your hand) or the carotid artery in your neck (next to your Adam's apple). Use the index and middle fingers of one hand to feel the pulse. If you use the artery in your neck, however, place your fingers gently; putting too much pressure on this artery can actually slow down your pulse and give you a false reading. When you've found your pulse, count the number of beats for ten seconds. Then multiply that number by six to find your heart rate in beats per minute. If you have trouble taking your pulse, you may want to purchase an inexpensive stethoscope that allows you to hear your heartbeat or use an automated pulse taker.

Another way to find your optimum level of exertion during exercise is to use your *maximum heart rate reserve*. Exercising at 50 percent to 85 percent of your maximum heart rate reserve will give you a healthy aerobic workout. This method is more precise than using a percent of your maximum heart rate (target heart rate range), but you'll need to do a little more calculating to figure it out. So we've outlined a simple formula that you can use to make it easier:

STEP ONE: Measure your resting heart rate by counting your pulse for ten seconds and multiplying that number by six. (Be sure to do this when you're resting.)

STEP TWO: Subtract your resting heart rate from your maximum heart rate. (Again, you can find your maximum heart rate by subtracting your age from 220 or by performing an exercise test.)

STEP THREE: Multiply the result of step two by .5 (50 percent) and add that to your resting heart rate to find the lower limit of your maximum heart rate reserve target zone.

STEP FOUR: Multiply the result of step two by .85 (85 percent) and add that to your resting heart rate to find the upper limit of your maximum heart rate reserve target zone.

You can use either of these methods as a guide throughout the walking programs in the next chapter. By exercising at 60 percent to 90 percent of your maximum heart rate or 50 percent to 85 percent of your maximum heart rate reserve for at least 20 minutes a day, 3 times a week or more, you can develop and maintain your aerobic fitness. Since freestyle walking is a moderately intense exercise, however, you may not be able to reach the upper limit of these ranges, according to Dr. Pollock, who helped draft the American College of Sports Medicine's *Guidelines for Fitness in Healthy Adults.* So you may have to walk longer (for at least 30 minutes) and more often (or progress to racewalking or walking with weights) to achieve the same benefit as you would by exercising at a higher heart rate.

As you'll see, the walking programs in this book are designed to get you to your optimum level of exercise gradually. At first, you'll walk at a comfortable pace, one that may not get your heart rate in the target zone. Then you will gradually work your heart rate into the target zone. By progressing slowly, you'll decrease your risk of injury. You'll also be more likely to stick with it. As your fitness increases, you will notice two telltale signs. It will take more exercise—or more intense exercise—to raise your heart rate into the target zone. And your resting heart rate will decline.

A word of caution: Don't be a slave to your pulse, measuring it so often that it becomes a compulsion. Don't let taking your pulse destroy your sense of fun and spontaneity in exercise. "We need to get away from the idea that if you don't bother calculating your heart rate, you're a failure," says Steven Blair, PED, director of epidemiology at the Institute for Aerobics Research in Dallas.

"Although we all agree that there is some minimum threshold, above which you must go to get some of these health benefits, we're not sure how low it is," he adds. "One reason we don't know is that most exercise training studies are pretty short-term, 10 or 20 weeks. Compared to a lifespan, that's very short."

When you first begin your walking program, you may want to take your pulse as often as every 10 or 15 minutes so that you can get a feel for how hard your body is working. As you progress through the program, you can take your pulse every 20 to 30 minutes to be sure you're working in your target range. In time, you may only need to check your pulse at the beginning and end of your walk; you may be able to tell whether you're working in your target range just by the way you feel.

As a matter of fact, one of the tools used by exercise scientists to measure and prescribe exercise is something called the rating of perceived exertion (RPE) scale. The exerciser rates how hard he or she feels the exercise is, using a 15-point scale that goes from 6 (resting) to 20 (very, very hard). This rating scale has been found to correlate well with physiological indicators of fatigue or strain, including heart rate and oxygen uptake. In other words, you can use your perception of how hard you're working as a guide. If you really feel like you're walking at a moderately intense pace, you probably are; a measurement of your heart rate would probably confirm that you're working in the moderately intense range of 50 percent to 75 percent of your maximum heart rate reserve. By checking your pulse more frequently during the early stages of your walking program, you'll get a feel for how your body reacts to different levels of exertion; later, you'll be able to judge your exertion without having to stop and check your pulse every ten minutes.

Listen To Your Body

There are three more principles that can guide you through your walking program. They should help you fight any tendency you may have to push yourself too hard. Remember, walking is an ideal activity to keep up for the rest of your life. You've got plenty of time to build up to a more demanding stride.

First is the "talk test," which is especially important during your first six weeks of walking. The talk test means that you should be able to hold a conversation with someone beside you as you walk. If you are too winded to talk, you can probably conclude that you're walking too fast for your present fitness level. Even if you walk alone, you can use your imagination. Do you feel like you could keep up a conversation? If not, you may want to slow down.

Second, your walk should be painless. If you experience a heaviness in your chest or any pain in your chest, jaw, neck, feet, legs, or back, you should slow down. If that doesn't stop the pain, see your doctor and describe what happened. Try to recall the circumstances: "I was walking up a hill," "It happened during the first few minutes," or "The weather was very cold."

Third, if you seem excessively tired for an hour or more after your walk, the walk was too strenuous. Your walk should be exhilarating, not fatiguing. If you experience a dizzy or lightheaded feeling, it's time to back off. If you feel like vomiting or are tired for at least a day after walking, take it easy. If you can't sleep at night or if your nerves seem shot, it means that you've been pushing too hard. The same is true if you seem to have lost your "zing" or can't catch your breath after a few minutes of walking. These are your body's warning signs. If you have any questions about excessive fatigue, pain, or discomfort, see your doctor.

All three of these points stress "listening" to your body. It may take some practice, but you'll probably find it fun. You'll really get to know your body. And you'll learn that your body really *can* tell you when to speed up or slow down.

Chapter 5

FREESTYLE FITNESS WALKING

Perhaps the best thing about walking is that you are already an expert at it. You probably acquired your walking skills when you were very young. If you're lucky, you've had plenty of opportunity to "practice" since then. In this chapter, however, we'll show you how to turn your walking skills into an exercise tool. With it, you'll be able to tune your body and improve your health.

The programs we've developed allow you to start out slowly and progress without strain, no matter how old you are or what shape you're in now. They're demanding enough to help you improve your fitness, but flexible enough for you to adapt them to your individual abilities and your daily routines. You can use them as a guide for a lifetime of freestyle walking or as a start-up step to get your body in gear for racewalking, walking with weights, or hiking. (See Chapters 6, 7, and 8 for more on these unique types of walking.)

Walking Style

The "secret" to walking comfortably is to walk naturally—pretty much as you've been walking up to now. Don't be too concerned with proper walking style for these freestyle walking programs. Remember, your body is unique. It has its own particular form and style, so you can't force it to behave exactly like someone else's body. Just walk naturally and enjoy yourself.

It is a good idea, however, to keep your spine straight and to hold your head high as you walk. You can walk into trouble—in the form of cars, trees, and other people—if you stare at the ground. Try not to be so conscious of your posture that you feel unnatural, though. Forget the ramrod-straight posture encouraged in the military, where the chest is thrown out and the back hyperextended. This posture doesn't allow your back and hips to move to accommodate the natural shift of your weight from one leg to the other as you walk. Instead, keep your wrists, hips, knees, and ankles relaxed. Allow your arms to hang loosely at your sides. They will swing naturally in opposite action to your legs—the left arm sweeping forward as the right leg strides ahead, and vice versa. (Racewalkers use a unique form that helps them to walk at high speeds. Refer to Chapter 6 if you would like to learn how to racewalk.)

As you walk, each foot should strike the ground at the heel. You then transfer your weight forward from your heel, along the outer portion of your foot, to your toes. To complete the foot-strike pattern, you push off with your toes. As you shift your weight from heel to toe, you should get a rolling motion. Avoid landing flat-footed or on the balls of your feet. If you do, you may be headed for some leg and foot problems later on. As you begin your walking program, don't worry about the length of your stride. Just do whatever is comfortable. As you increase your speed, your stride length will increase as well.

Breathe naturally as you walk, using both your nose and your mouth. Remember that the faster you go the more air you'll need. So help yourself to all the air you want.

Don't follow these guidelines slavishly. It's likely that the way you walk now is best for you. However, if you do experience any pain or discomfort while you walk, you may need to make an adjustment in your walking technique or switch to a different pair of walking shoes. You'll find more about walking pain and its various causes in Chapter 10. If you have further questions, see your doctor. Remember, you're not in a beauty contest. You're walking for fun and fitness.

Warming Up and Cooling Down

As with any exercise program, each workout in your walking program should start with a warm-up period and end with a cool-down period. You can achieve this by starting each walking workout with five minutes of slow walking, followed by a series of stretches. Then, after walking at your regular pace, end your workout with a five-minute slow walk, followed by another series of stretches. (See Chapter 9 for more on warming up, cooling down, and stretching.) These steps are essential parts of your walking program. They will help you maintain your flexibility and prevent pain or injury. Warming up, cooling down, and stretching all become even more important if you graduate to more demanding workouts that involve striding, racewalking, using weights, or walking up or down hills. The greater intensity of these workouts increases your risk of injuring tight muscles.

How to Get Started

To get yourself started and keep yourself walking, you need a plan that puts you on a regular walking schedule. We're now going to take you step-by-step through a program that works. It will help you increase your health and fitness while you experience the true pleasures of walking. You'll find this program demanding enough to get the job done, yet flexible enough to be adapted to your particular needs, age, present level of fitness, and life-style.

Getting started doesn't require any elaborate planning or expensive equipment—just a comfortable pair of well-constructed walking shoes to support and cushion your feet and prevent them from turning inward too much when they hit the ground. (See Chapter 15 about what to look for in walking shoes.) Don't forget to warm up and stretch before you actually hit the trail.

Basic Starter Program

The CONSUMER GUIDE® Basic Starter Program is a good way to prepare your body for more demanding exercise. If you find the Basic Starter Program too difficult or if you have heart, lung, or joint problems, you should begin with the Special Starter Program on page 80. If you are recovering from a heart attack, turn to the special cardiac programs beginning on page 83.

The following table summarizes the Basic Starter Program.

Level 1: Walk 20 minutes a day 3 to 5 times a week.

Level 2: Walk 25 minutes a day 3 to 5 times a week.

Level 3: Walk 30 minutes a day 3 to 5 times a week.

Level 4: Walk 35 minutes a day 3 to 5 times a week.

Level 5: Walk 40 minutes a day 3 to 5 times a week.

Level 6: Walk 45 minutes a day 3 to 5 times a week.

In this starter program, you should walk fast enough to get your heart rate into the lower end of your target zone—about 60 percent of your maximum heart rate or about 50 percent of your maximum heart rate reserve (See Chapter 4 to learn how to find your target heart rate). If you find that you can't walk comfortably at that pace for the specified amount of time, then slow down. Stay at each level until you can keep your heart rate in the lower end of your target zone for the specified amount of time, then proceed to the next level. The key is always to listen to your body. You may need to spend two weeks at each level, or maybe a week at one level and two weeks at another. Whatever works best for you is fine as long as you spend at least a week at each level. If, however, you find that walking at even a very slow pace for 20 minutes is too difficult for you, then switch to the Special Starter Program.

Try not to get impatient and skip ahead, even if you find the Basic Starter Program too easy. Stick with it— slow and steady. You'll be glad you did, because this approach will raise the odds that you'll continue with your walking program. Many people "attack" a fitness program, and quit after just a few weeks. Remember, anybody can start an exercise program, but not everyone can stay with it. Your primary goal in this starter program is to get motivated to exercise on a regular basis. Once you've completed it, you can proceed to the Basic Walking Program.

Special Starter Program

The CONSUMER GUIDE® Special Starter Program is designed for people who find the Basic Starter Program too difficult or who have serious health problems. Those who are recovering from a heart attack, however, should try one of the special cardiac programs. The following table summarizes the Special Starter Program.

Level 1: Walk 10 minutes a day 3 to 5 times a week.

Level 2: Walk 12 minutes a day 3 to 5 times a week.

Level 3: Walk 14 minutes a day 3 to 5 times a week.

Level 4: Walk 16 minutes a day 3 to 5 times a week.

Level 5: Walk 18 minutes a day 3 to 5 times a week.

Level 6: Walk 20 minutes a day 3 to 5 times a week.

In the Special Starter Program, you should begin by walking at a comfortable pace, even if it doesn't elicit your target heart rate. Begin at a level that feels comfortable and stay there for at least one week, then proceed to the next level.

If, however, the Level 1 duration of ten minutes, three to five times a week is too difficult—for instance, if you're out of breath as you walk—then start by walking five minutes a day or less. Some emphysema patients walk for only a minute or two at the start. You must be the judge.

Once you can walk without discomfort for 20 minutes a day, 3 to 5 times a week, move on to the Basic Starter Program. From there, you will eventually graduate to the Basic Walking Program.

Basic Walking Program

Once you've completed the Basic Starter Program, you are ready for bigger and better things, including walking faster and getting your heart rate well into your target range. Now it's time to begin the Basic Walking Program, summarized in the following table.

Level 1: Walk 20 minutes a day 3 to 5 times a week.

Level 2: Walk 25 minutes a day 3 to 5 times a week.

Level 3: Walk 30 minutes a day 3 to 5 times a week.

Level 4: Walk 35 minutes a day 3 to 5 times a week.

Level 5: Walk 40 minutes a day 3 to 5 times a week.

Level 6: Walk 45 minutes a day 3 to 5 times a week.

Level 7: Walk 50 minutes a day 3 to 5 times a week.

Level 8: Walk 55 minutes a day 3 to 5 times a week.

Level 9: Walk 60 minutes a day 3 to 5 times a week.

In the Basic Walking Program, your aim is to get your heart pumping at 70 percent to 80 percent of your maximum heart rate or 60 percent to 75 percent of your maximum heart rate reserve. Of course, as your fitness increases, you can't expect to just shuffle along and reach this heart rate range. You'll have to walk at a good clip.

As in the Basic Starter Program, you need to stay at each level until you can walk at that pace for the specified amount of time.

Once you've reached Level 9 (or Level 6 if you're short on time) of this program, you can maintain your fitness level by walking in your target range for at least 30 to 45 minutes a day, at least 3 times a week.

While these programs provide guidelines for how much exercise you need to do to improve your health and fitness, your own fitness goals can help you choose the exact duration, frequency, and speed of your walks. For instance, if your main goal is to lose weight, you may choose to walk for 45 minutes to an hour, 5 times a week, at 65 percent to 70 percent of your maximum heart rate. By keeping to a more moderate pace (yet still in your target zone), you'll be able to walk for a longer period of time. And as discussed in Chapter 1, by walking for a longer period of time, you'll burn more calories.

There's a simple rule of thumb to follow: If you decrease the speed of your walks, increase their duration and frequency. You can adjust how often, how long, and how fast you walk to suit your goals, as long as you keep your heart rate somewhere within your target zone and exercise for a minimum of 30 minutes a day, at least 3 times a week.

If you find yourself missing the slower pace of the starter program and the chance it gave you to savor your surroundings, you may want to alternate brisk walks with more leisurely ones. You might try confining brisk walking to 30 minutes or so in the middle of your workout, sandwiched between long, slow warm-up and cooldown periods. You may also want to walk up and down hilly terrain, so that you can increase the intensity of your workout without having to walk at high speeds.

Of course, you don't have to restrict your walking to your "official" workout times. Instead, you can try taking full advantage of the opportunities that each day offers for extra walking. For instance, try walking up and down stairs at every chance you get, instead of taking an elevator or escalator. (For more ideas on how to fit more walking into your day, see Chapter 13.) Remember, any walking you can do in addition to your scheduled workouts is an added bonus in terms of health and fitness.

For the sake of convenience, it is important to build your walks into your daily schedule of activities (see Chapter 13). To keep your motivation high and your walks interesting, you may want to vary the routes you choose to roam (see Chapter 12) or add new dimensions to your walking routine (see Chapter 14).

Once you have mastered the Basic Starter Program and the Basic Walking Program, you may decide you want more challenge. Or you may be so fit that you have trouble walking fast enough to push your heart rate well into your target zone. If so, you can increase the intensity of your workouts by learning to racewalk (see Chapter 6), which will enable you to reach higher walking speeds, or using weights as you walk (see Chapter 7). You may also want to try increasing the time and distance you walk by taking up hiking (see Chapter 8).

Special Cardiac Programs

If you are recovering from a heart attack, walking may be able to help you down the road to recovery. Cardiac Program 1 is a walking program you can use if you have had a heart attack and have your doctor's permission to exercise. This program assumes that your recovery is normal and uncomplicated. You *must* go over this program with your doctor before you begin. Your doctor must establish your target heart rate. This will be done through an exercise test. The test will indicate how high your heart rate may safely go. Your doctor must also explain what you should do if you experience any discomfort and how to take your medication (if your condition requires medication).

Cardiac Program 1

Level 1: Walk 3 to 5 minutes 5 times a week.

Level 2: Walk 6 to 8 minutes 5 times a week.

Level 3: Walk 9 to 11 minutes 5 times a week.

Level 4: Walk 12 to 14 minutes 5 times a week.

Level 5: Walk 15 to 17 minutes 5 times a week.

Level 6: Walk 18 to 20 minutes 5 times a week.

Level 7: Walk 20 minutes 3 to 5 times a week.

Level 8: Walk 25 minutes 3 to 5 times a week.

Level 9: Walk 30 minutes 3 to 5 times a week.

Level 10: Walk 35 minutes 3 to 5 times a week.

Level 11: Walk 40 minutes 3 to 5 times a week.

Level 12: Walk 45 minutes 3 to 5 times a week.

Level 13: Walk 50 minutes 3 to 5 times a week.

Level 14: Walk 55 minutes 3 to 5 times a week.

Level 15: Walk 60 minutes 3 to 5 times a week.

If you have had a heart attack and get fatigued easily, have claudication (blockage of circulation in the legs), or get leg cramps, you may be able to use Cardiac Program 2. This walking program should be followed in a medically supervised class, unless your doctor directs you otherwise. Once again, you *must* discuss this program with your doctor. Your doctor must establish your target heart rate before you begin and explain what you should do if you experience discomfort. During the one-minute "rest" periods, you can walk slower, stand in place and move your feet, or sit down and wiggle your toes (you want to continue some type of movement to keep blood circulating in your legs).

Cardiac Program 2

Level 1: Walk 1 minute, rest 1 minute,

walk 1 minute, rest 1 minute,

walk 1 minute, rest 1 minute,

walk 1 minute.   *5 times a week*

Level 2: Walk 1 minute, rest 1 minute,

walk 2 minutes, rest 1 minute,

walk 2 minutes, rest 1 minute,

walk 1 minute.   *5 times a week*

Level 3: Walk 1 minute, rest 1 minute,

walk 3 minutes, rest 1 minute,

walk 3 minutes, rest 1 minute,

walk 1 minute.   *5 times a week*

Level 4: Walk 1 minute, rest 1 minute,

walk 5 minutes, rest 1 minute,

walk 5 minutes, rest 1 minute,

walk 1 minute.   *5 times a week*

Level 5: Walk 1 minute, rest 1 minute,

walk 7 minutes, rest 1 minute,

walk 7 minutes, rest 1 minute,

walk 1 minute.   *5 times a week*

Level 6: Walk 1 minute, rest 1 minute,

walk 8 minutes, rest 1 minute,

walk 8 minutes, rest 1 minute,

walk 1 minute.   *5 times a week*

Level 7: Walk 1 minute, rest 1 minute,

walk 9 minutes, rest 1 minute,

walk 9 minutes, rest 1 minute,

walk 1 minute.   *5 times a week*

Level 8: Walk 1 minute, rest 1 minute,

walk 10 minutes, rest 1 minute,

walk 10 minutes, rest 1 minute,

walk 1 minute.   *3 to 5 times a week*

Level 9: Walk 1 minute, rest 1 minute,

walk 11 minutes, rest 1 minute,

walk 11 minutes, rest 1 minute,

walk 1 minute.   *3 to 5 times a week*

Level 10: Walk 1 minute, rest 1 minute,

walk 12 minutes, rest 1 minute,

walk 12 minutes, rest 1 minute,

walk 1 minute.   *3 to 5 times a week*

Level 11: Walk 1 minute, rest 1 minute,

walk 14 minutes, rest 1 minute,

walk 14 minutes, rest 1 minute,

walk 1 minute.   *3 to 5 times a week*

Level 12: Walk 1 minute, rest 1 minute,

walk 16 minutes, rest 1 minute,

walk 16 minutes, rest 1 minute,

walk 1 minute.   *3 to 5 times a week*

Level 13: Walk 1 minute, rest 1 minute,

walk 18 minutes, rest 1 minute,

walk 18 minutes, rest 1 minute,

walk 1 minute.   *3 to 5 times a week*

Level 14: Walk 1 minute, rest 1 minute,

walk 20 minutes, rest 1 minute,

walk 20 minutes, rest 1 minute,

walk 1 minute.   *3 to 5 times a week*

With your doctor's approval, you can progress to Level 7 of Cardiac Program 1 when you reach Level 14 of this program.

Chapter 6

RACEWALKING

Once you've worked your way through the freestyle Starter and Walking Programs in Chapter 5, you may well be interested in accelerating your program to get even more of an aerobic workout. Perhaps you feel the need for speed. Or maybe you're craving competition. If so, learning to racewalk may be a natural next step for you. By using the technique of racewalking, you'll be able to go faster and raise your heart rate well into the target range, even if you are already quite fit.

Why Racewalk?

Racewalking maximizes the workout that walking can provide. The reason is that at racewalking speeds of five miles per hour or more, it is actually more efficient for your body to jog than to walk. You can experience this for yourself: Try walking as fast as you can, and you'll feel your body aching to jog. In order to continue walking and not break into a jog, you have to keep one foot on the ground at all times. You can't use that gliding motion—when both feet are off the ground—that allows joggers to cover more distance with each step. So in order to cover the same distance, you end up having to take more steps than you would if you were jogging.

Therefore, at these high speeds, racewalking actually involves a higher rate of muscle activity and burns more calories per mile than does jogging at the same pace. According to Dr. James Rippe of the University of Massachusetts, racewalking burns 120 to 130 calories per mile—that's more than running, which burns between 100 and 110, and certainly more than freestyle walking.

Racewalking also gives your upper body a healthy workout. In order to walk at high speeds, you have to pump your arms vigorously. This movement helps tone and strengthen the muscles in your arms, neck, and chest, as it burns calories.

All this extra activity shows up in increased health and fitness benefits. Indeed, elite competitive racewalkers have physiological profiles that are comparable to those of distance runners. They have low body fat and a high ratio of "good" to "bad" cholesterol, according to a study conducted at Wayne State University, in Detroit.

Another advantage of racewalking is that it can be practiced as a competitive sport. You can compete against others, not just against your own performance. It's an excellent way to add challenge to your walking program. Racewalking is even an Olympic event. That doesn't mean you have to be Olympic material to try your hand at it, though. Racewalking can also be practiced and enjoyed without entering any competitions.

Racewalking does put greater stress on the ankle, knee, and hip joints than does freestyle walking (whenever you increase the intensity of an exercise, you increase the risk of injury). But the strain is less than that caused by jogging, because you always have one foot on the ground when you racewalk. You can hold down your risk of injury by beginning your program slowly and increasing your speed gradually; by doing plenty of stretches and allowing your body to warm up before you begin each walk; and by following proper racewalking form.

Proper Racewalking Form

You may have seen racewalkers on television or watched them "wiggle" past you in the local park. You may have wondered at their unusual technique—vigorously pumping arms and exaggerated hip action. Some people find it comical, but racewalkers know that it's this unique form that allows them to reach high walking speeds.

Racewalkers generally walk at speeds ranging from about five miles per hour to about nine miles per hour (walking at speeds of five miles per hour or more without using the racewalking technique is very difficult, if not impossible, for most people). Record-setting elite racewalkers, however, have achieved astounding speeds nearing ten-and-one-half miles per hour—that's just a tad under a six-minute mile! But especially when you are just starting out with racewalking, it is important to concentrate more on the proper form, which is no cinch to master, than on speed. Speed will come later, as you master the technique.

There are three main features of racewalking form; they're in the official rules that govern the sport. Those rules, according to the International Amateur Athletic Federation, say that: 1) One foot must be in contact with

Racewalking Form

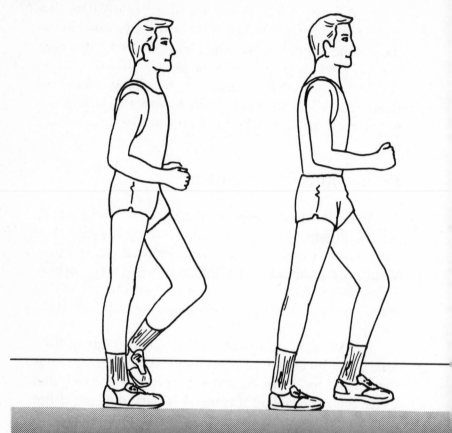

As the body passes over the torso, the supporting leg is straight in the upright position. The opposite leg is moving forward, with the foot close to the ground. Note that the arm is bent at a 90 degree angle.

The supporting leg is beginning to push the body ahead, causing the body to lean forward slightly. The opposite hip and leg are swinging forward, with the foot close to the ground. The arm above the supporting leg is beginning its upward thrust.

The supporting leg is exerting a strong push as the body leans forward. The opposite hip and leg are reaching forward. The arm above the supporting leg is pumping across the chest as the opposite arm pumps back.

The supporting leg continues to push the body forward as the heel of the opposite foot touches the ground. Note that the foot of the supporting leg is still in contact with the ground as the back of the opposite heel makes contact. The arms are at the high point of their pumping motion.

the ground at all times. 2) There must be a two-leg support period during each cycle of pushing off, swinging, and weight acceptance. and 3) The weight-supporting leg must be straight for at least one moment when it's in the vertically upright position. In other words, you must have one foot touching the ground at all times. The heel of your front foot must touch the ground before the toes of your back foot leave the ground. And, during your stride, the leg that is supporting your weight must be straight for a least a moment as your torso passes directly over it.

How do you adjust your form to incorporate these features? Stand straight, with your toes aimed dead ahead. Begin walking by stepping forward with your left hip, your left knee, and your left heel. Be sure you land first on the back edge of your heel. Your left foot should be at a 90 degree angle to your left leg (your leg and foot should form the shape of a capital "L"), and your heel should be at about a 40 degree angle to the ground. When the back edge of your heel strikes, tilt your foot ever-so-slightly toward the outer edge of your shoe; you'll be rolling on the outer edge of your foot as you shift your weight from the back to the front of your foot. This will keep your knee from rotating inward, which can cause "runner's knee."

As your left leg lands and begins to pull you forward, give yourself a strong pushoff with your right foot. As your right foot leaves the ground and begins to swing forward, your torso will pass directly over your left leg. At that moment, your left leg must be straight. Once your torso has passed directly over your left leg, your left leg will push you forward until the back of your right heel strikes the ground.

You should keep a few things in mind as you practice this technique. First, be sure to keep your toes pointing straight ahead as you walk. If you don't, you'll be moving from side to side as well as forward, wasting energy and losing speed.

Second, pay attention to foot placement. In freestyle walking, your feet land about shoulder-width apart (in the side-to-side direction). In racewalking, your feet should line up one behind the other. To practice this, try walking an imaginary straight line (or draw a straight line on the pavement with chalk). As you extend each leg forward, try to plant it on the line, or as close to the line as possible. This will keep you from waddling and give you a smooth, efficient stride.

Third, when your supporting leg is straight, the hip above it should rise and relax. This will let the bones of the leg support the weight and give the muscles a break. This hip movement can be somewhat hard to achieve at first, particularly for men who are "trained" to believe that mobile hips are feminine-looking. But the hip movement is crucial to the racewalker, because it makes the stride as smooth as possible. Also, as you swing the non-supporting leg forward, be sure to swing the hip above it forward, too.

Finally, as you walk, you should feel yourself leaning forward from the ankles. Don't bend forward at the waist, however. This will strain your back and neck, and hamper your breathing.

In addition to using your legs and hips correctly, you need to get your arms in on the act. As in freestyle walking, your arms will naturally swing to counterbalance your legs. But if you consciously and vigorously pump your arms, you can actually help your legs move faster. To get the most benefit, keep your arms bent at right angles. Pump them diagonally across the center of your body, keeping your elbows close to your sides. Don't pump them too high, however—chest-high is enough.

As you incorporate all of these movements into your form, you probably will be walking at a fairly slow pace. That's fine for this stage. Just walk at a pace that's comfortable and focus on your form. Once you feel comfortable with these movements, you can begin to increase your speed and raise your heart rate into your target zone. Be sure, however, to increase your speed gradually. Don't push too hard or walk to the point of exhaustion.

Stretching

Before you begin each workout, even those in the early stage when you're just practicing your form, you need to warm up your body and stretch your muscles. The same goes for after each workout. If you neglect these important preparations, you may be in for some serious pain and perhaps even injury.

Before you begin your racewalking workout, walk slowly and casually (not in racewalking form) for a few minutes to warm up your muscles. Then stop and stretch. In Chapter 9, you'll find various stretches to choose from. Stretches that involve the upper and lower body are important, because so many of the body's muscles are involved in racewalking. Stretch your muscles gently, without bouncing or pulling to the point of pain. Once you've completed your walk, stretch again to help maintain your flexibility.

Even with proper stretching, you may feel some soreness early in the program. That's to be expected, since you may not have used some of those muscles in a while. (Be sure to pamper your muscles with massages and warm baths.) Don't walk to the point of pain, however. If pain or discomfort persists, see your doctor.

Since racewalking is such a specialized activity, and so distinct from freestyle walking and jogging, some shoes have been designed specifically for racewalking. See Chapter 15 for more about these.

Entering Competition

A large number of local, national, and international racewalking competitions are held each year, covering distances from 1 mile to 31 miles (50 kilometers). These events allow you the opportunity to test out your speed *and* your form.

Unlike running races and marathons, racewalking competitions are judged for form. The judges will give you a warning if your form is not correct (for instance, if your back foot leaves the ground before your front foot touches). After three warnings, you can be disqualified.

You could, of course, enter running races or marathons and racewalk your way through. This way, you wouldn't be judged on technique, but you would still be competing. As you increase your speed and skill, you may even find yourself passing some of the runners, especially in longer events.

Whichever type of competition you choose, it's best to begin with shorter, slower races. Stay away from very short sprinting races, however; you might be tempted to push yourself too hard too soon. You may want to try a more moderately paced four-mile event first. In order to progress to longer or faster races, you'll need to prepare yourself—increasing your speed and distance gradually in your training sessions.

Before you begin entering races, you may want to attend a racewalking event as a spectator. By watching the competitors, you may be able to pick up tips for perfecting your form. You may also want to ask the racers or judges for advice on proper form.

Chapter 7

WALKING WITH WEIGHTS

How can you increase the fitness benefits you get from the freestyle walking programs in Chapter 5? Try putting on some weights. By wearing or carrying weights, you can boost walking's energy costs to those of a jog—even when you walk at moderate speeds. And if you choose wrist or hand weights, you can strengthen and tone the muscles in your upper body at the same time.

Walking with weights is a good way to get a hearty workout if you find fast walking uncomfortable. It's also a useful option if you simply prefer moderately paced walks that allow you to take in the sights. On the other hand, if you enjoy racewalking, you can combine weights and speed for a vigorous total body workout (However, jogging with weights can be dangerous because of the greater strain this combination puts on the feet, legs, and spine).

Weighted Benefits

Once you have progressed through the starter and basic walking programs (see Chapter 5) and can walk comfortably at four miles per hour, you can use weights to increase the benefits you get from each of your workouts. By adding weights, you can burn more calories at a given speed than you would without them. The reason is simple; it takes more energy to move more weight. That's why a heavier person burns more calories per mile than a slimmer person walking at the same speed.

In a study conducted at the University of Louisville, in Kentucky, people who walked with hand or ankle weights at four miles per hour were able to boost their exercise intensity to the equivalent of jogging at five miles per hour without weights. When they walked at four miles per hour wearing *both* hand and ankle weights, they expended *more* calories then they did when they jogged at five miles per hour without weights. However, the study indicated that the use of ankle weights alone did not require as much energy as did the use of hand weights alone.

To move more weight your muscles must work harder. For this extra work, your muscles need more oxygen. A study performed by Leonard Schwartz, M.D., and his colleagues at the University of Pittsburgh showed that adding hand-weighted arm movements significantly increased the amount of oxygen consumed in walking. The increase in oxygen consumption ranged from 13 percent to 155 percent, depending on the speed of the walks, the amount of arm movement, and how much weight was held in the hands (weights ranged from one pound to five pounds). The faster the speed, the wider the range of arm movement, and the heavier the weights, the more oxygen the weighted walking demanded.

To meet this demand for extra oxygen, your heart must beat faster. That's why walking with weights can help you get your heart rate well into your target zone, even if you're already quite fit. In a study conducted by Dr. Michael Pollock of the University of Florida, walkers increased their working heart rates by as many as 12 beats per minute by pumping three-pound weights as they walked.

Using hand-held or wrist-wrapped weights can also help you build your upper body as you walk. By vigorously pumping your weighted arms, you can strengthen and tone the muscles in your chest, shoulders, and arms. These movements will also add to your calorie burn and help increase your heart rate, giving you a challenging total body workout.

How to Use Weights

If you decide to try walking with weights, remember this simple rule: Start slow and light, then raise intensity bit by bit. Just as in freestyle walking, you'll need to gauge how hard you're working by taking your pulse (see Chapter 4) and listening to your body. The intensity of your workouts will depend not only on how much weight you use, but on which type of weights you use, how you use them, and how fast you walk.

You have several types and styles of weights to choose from for your walking program, including weights that you can hold in your hands, wear around your wrists, tie onto your shoes, wrap around your ankles, or wear on your torso. If you decide to hold the weight in your hands, you can pick up a set of small, light dumbbells. Another option is hand-held weights that have a strap or padded bar that fits around the back of your hand to help you hold on to the weight. Also available are hollow, plastic containers, shaped like small dumbbells, that can be filled with water or sand. They provide versatility because you can adjust the amount of weight you carry by adding or spilling out liquid or sand. They also provide a handy way to carry drinking water for your walks.

Wrist weights also come in several styles. Some are wrapped in foam and covered with vinyl, others are wrapped in padded terry cloth. Some are made of elastic material that allows you to slip the weight over your hand and onto your wrist, while others strap on like a watchband.

Wrist-wrapped and hand-held weights—used alone or with ankle weights—appear to offer the greatest rewards. They help build the upper body as they increase the aerobic benefits of walking. With hand or wrist weights, you can increase the intensity of your walks in three ways: 1) by adding more weight; 2) by moving your arms more vigorously; or 3) by walking faster.

Your pace, at first, should be slow and comfortable. Don't worry too much about getting your heart rate into your target zone until you've given your body a chance to adjust to the added weight. Then you can build the intensity of your workouts by gradually stepping up to a more moderate pace.

While using hand or wrist weights, you'll want to work up to pumping your arms vigorously, like a racewalker. Pumping your arms pays off by boosting your heart rate much more than merely carrying the weight does. Vigorous arm movements also help to tone the muscles in your upper body.

When you begin, simply let your arms swing in opposition to your legs. Then gradually put more force into your arm swings. As these movements become easier, try really pumping your arms. Keep your elbows bent at

90 degree angles and pump each arm across your chest as the opposite leg moves forward. Your arm movements should be as smooth and controlled as possible—not abrupt or marked by jerking motions.

The higher you pump your arms and the more effort you put into your movements, the higher your heart rate will go. Be careful not to pump your arms too high, however. "Chest or shoulder height is the highest the arms should swing," warns Dr. Pollock. If you go higher than that, you risk pulling muscles in your arms or injuring your elbows.

In terms of weight, begin with one pound on each wrist or in each hand. Stay at this weight level until the weight begins to feel too light. Remember that you'll be trying to pump the weights. So it may take two or three weeks or more before you're ready to add to your load. Then you can gradually add more weight, in half-pound or one-pound increments, up to a maximum of three pounds per arm. "Above three pounds, we've noticed that 'tennis elbow' becomes a problem," says Dr. Pollock. Tennis elbow is a painful and sometimes disabling inflammation of the muscle and tissues of the elbow.

Carrying groceries or a briefcase while walking may exert some of the same effects as hand-held weights, although this has not been studied. Hand and wrist weights have been found to be most advantageous when they are pumped up and down, however. And since people carrying groceries or briefcases tend not to pump their arms, the effects on heart rate and calorie burn are likely to be significantly less impressive using these makeshift weights.

An alternative to using hand or wrist weights is trying weights that wrap around the ankles or lace directly onto your shoes. Ankle weights generally come in styles similar to those for wrist weights; they can either be strapped on or slipped over your foot. Weights designed to be worn on your shoes have small holes so that you can slip them onto your laces and tie them in place. They often come in sets, with each weight weighing half a pound. The set provides versatility because you can start out with one weight on each shoe and gradually add weights as you progress through the program and build your strength.

Unlike hand-held or wrist-wrapped weights, ankle weights won't do anything for your upper-body strength. But they can greatly enhance the action of walking in toning up your leg muscles, including the calf muscles, hamstrings, hip flexors, and quadriceps. To increase the intensity of your workouts as you use ankle weights, you'll need to gradually add more weight or walk faster.

As with hand-held and wrist weights, it is important to start light, with no more than a half-pound weight on each ankle, even if you are already very fit. Build up gradually by adding another half-pound every three weeks, but don't use more than three pounds on each ankle or foot.

Carrying weight on your torso—in the form of a backpack, a weighted belt, or a weighted vest—is another option. The belts and vests often have compartments for weights, so you can adjust your load simply by adding or removing weights. And, of course, you can easily adjust the amount of weight you carry in the backpack by adding or removing items. Wearing these types of weights during routine fitness walking is a good way for hikers to prepare themselves for longer hikes or backpacking trips.

These weights, however, won't tone the arms the way hand weights will. And although wearing weights on the torso does raise the caloric cost of walking at a given speed—up to 10 percent, for weights totalling 10 to

40 percent of body weight—it does so to a much lesser extent than does using weights on the ankles, hands, or wrists, according to a study conducted at the University of Massachusetts. (See Chapter 8 on hiking and back-packing.) If you do decide to try these types of weights, the rule to follow, once again, is "Start slow and light, then raise intensity bit by bit."

No matter which type of weights you choose, be sure to pay attention to how your feet strike the ground. As in freestyle walking and racewalking, your heel should make contact first. You should shift your weight gradually toward the front of your foot. And your toes should be the last part of your foot to leave the ground.

To prevent injuries with weighted walking, it is particularly important to make sure you warm up, cool down, and stretch adequately (see Chapter 9). If you use hand-held, wrist-wrapped, or torso weights, you'll be working muscles in your upper body that probably didn't get much of a workout in your freestyle walking program. So stretches and exercises that emphasize the neck, back, shoulders, chest, and arms are essential before and after your workouts with these weights. Also, before you begin your weighted walking program, be sure to read the safety section that follows and check with your doctor if you have any questions about your ability to use weights.

Safety

Walking with weights is certainly not for everyone. For instance, it is definitely not for a beginning walker who has been inactive for a long time. If you want to try walking with weights, be sure to work your way through the freestyle starter and basic walking programs in Chapter 5 first.

Although it appears to be safer for the ankles, knees, and hips than jogging, weighted walking does put a bit more stress on the joints than freestyle walking does. This joint-stressing drawback is more pronounced for ankle-wrapped or shoe-laced weights than for wrist-wrapped or hand-held ones. And walking with a back-pack or weighted belt or vest puts even more stress on the joints—and on the back.

According to Dr. Kevin Campbell of the Cleveland Clinic, people with back problems should be wary not only of carrying backpacks and weighted belts and vests, but even of using hand and wrist weights. A natural part of walking, he says, is that the upper body rotates in an opposite direction to the lower body. At the end of a stride, the back muscles carry the burden of stopping the rotation in one direction and starting the opposite rotation. Because hand and wrist weights, like torso-carried weights, increase the upper body's inertia, they make the back muscles work harder to reverse the direction of the rotation.

Some researchers, including Dr. Pollock, have questioned the safety of walking with hand-held weights, particularly for people who have high blood pressure—and even for those with normal resting blood pressure that surges in response to exercise. The reason: They have noticed that walkers have a disproportionate rise in blood pressure while they are using hand-held weights.

However, the phenomenon has been explained, and with the explanation comes a simple solution, says Dr. Pollock. The hand gripping is what makes blood pressure go up. It seems that whenever people clench their hands, their blood pressure rises in an exaggerated fashion.

The solution to this apparent safety problem, according to Dr. Pollock, is to learn to relax your hands as much as possible when you are carrying or pumping hand-held weights. An even better move is to switch to a weight designed to wrap around your wrist. With wrist weights, you don't need to grip at all, so the blood pressure concern disappears.

If you have any health problems, including high blood pressure or problems with your joints, elbows, or back, be sure to consult your doctor before trying weighted walking. If you—or your doctor—are concerned about the possible safety hazards associated with weighted walking, consider this alternative. You can achieve some of the same strengthening and toning benefits that come from walking with weights simply by splitting the activities in two. You can keep up your freestyle walking or racewalking program, without weights. Then, on days when you're not walking, visit a gymnasium or health club (or, if you can afford it, a home gym), where you can develop a program of high-repetition, low-weight training, that will help you strengthen your muscles, especially those in your upper body.

Chapter 8

HIKING

Stepping up your pace is one way to build the intensity of your workouts. But as discussed in Chapter 5, if walking quickly is too uncomfortable, you can opt for longer walks at a more moderate pace. Hiking is a pleasurable way to make this trade. In terms of energy costs, a day-long hike up hills and down winding paths is similar to running a marathon. However, when it comes to taking in the sights, smells, and sounds as you go, hiking is tough to beat.

Where to Go

Where you choose to hike will depend, in part, on your interests. If you enjoy watching birds, for example, you may want to pack your binoculars and head for a swampy area like the Everglades National Park, which is known for its ornithological richness. If you're interested in plant life, you may want to plan a spring or summer hike in the Great Smoky Mountains National Park, where you'll find a brilliant display of rhododendrons and azaleas. If you just want to get out into nature, you may want to join the 20 million hikers and backpackers who put the national and state parks to good use each year.

You don't have to plan a cross-country trip, however, to take a hike. Chances are you'll find a national, state, or local park in your area that offers scenic trails for hiking. Trail maps are often available to guide you; some show estimates of mileage and may indicate the degree of difficulty of the trails. To find out more about national parks in your area, contact the National Park Service (see Appendix). Your state board of tourism may be able to provide you with information about state and local parks. Local chapters of hiking groups and environmental organizations may also be able to assist you.

You may be asking yourself, "When am I going to find time to get to a national park for a hiking trip?" But hikes don't have to be excursions into the deepest wilds and they don't always require weeks or months of planning. Even if you live in an urban area, you'll probably be able to find forest or wildlife preserves nearby that you can roam in for a few hours. They may not look all that challenging as you pass them in your car, but getting out on your own two feet and exploring them close up can be an invigorating experience. It's a healthy and inexpensive way to escape the noise and traffic of the city. It's also a good way to prepare your body for lengthier hikes across rougher terrain.

Preparing Yourself

Before you head out on the wilderness trail, you'll need to condition your body for the greater intensity of hiking. Once you've completed the starter and basic walking programs in Chapter 5, you should be able to walk comfortably on level ground for four or five miles at a time. If you can't, you'll need to stay with the freestyle program and gradually increase the distance you walk until you can.

Rarely will you find a hiking path that's smooth and level. So you'll need to prepare your body for tackling hilly terrain. To do this, choose a four- or five-mile route near your home that has plenty of inclines. Since walking up and down inclines takes more energy than walking on level ground, you may have to begin at a pace that's slightly slower than your usual walking speed. Walk the entire length of this route three or four times a week for several weeks, until you can manage it comfortably at a moderate pace.

Your next step is to practice walking on hilly terrain with weight on your back. Even if you'll be sticking to short day hikes, you'll probably need to carry a few things with you. So fill your hiking pack with items you're likely to take on short trips, including a filled canteen, a small first aid kit, a raincoat or poncho, a sweatshirt, and some snacks. Then walk that four- or five-mile hilly stretch near your home a few times a week for several weeks.

Once you've completed this round of conditioning, you should be ready for a day hike. You'll need to successfully complete a few day hikes—and practice walking with a heavier pack—before you'll be ready for an overnight trip. For your first hike, choose a well-marked trail that you can cover at a moderate pace in less than a day.

As you hike, choose a comfortable pace. You'll be walking for several hours, so don't race through the first mile. Be sure to give yourself rest stops, too. You may want to try stopping for about ten minutes each hour. More frequent breaks may cause you to lose momentum. If you absolutely need to rest a little more often, however, by all means do.

What to Wear

When you start out on a hike, it's better to be wearing too much than too little. You'll want to be prepared for the worst even if the weather is beautiful when you begin. Of course, you probably don't need to carry your snow gear for a mid-July walk through low altitudes. You will, however, want to wear or carry clothes that will protect you from rain, winds, and a sudden drop in temperature. Keep in mind that shady areas can be much cooler than sunny spots.

Dress yourself in several thin layers. This way, you can strip off layers if you feel too warm. Choose a soft material that absorbs sweat (like cotton) for the layer next to your skin. For your outer layer, try a light, breathable windbreaker. If you haven't included it as one of your layers, toss a sweater (or sweatshirt) into your pack.

Even if rain doesn't look probable, it's best to come equipped with rain gear. In wet weather, a wet hiker can become frostbitten and hypothermic, even if the temperature isn't all that low. (See Chapter 11 for tips on dressing for cold and wet weather.) A large, foldable poncho that will protect you and your pack is a wise choice.

You'll also need a sturdy, comfortable pair of hiking boots or walking shoes designed for off-road terrain. For information on choosing hiking boots, see Chapter 15. Be sure to break them in gradually by wearing them around the house before you take them on the road.

You can find out more about preparing yourself for all kinds of weather by reading Chapter 11. You'll also learn how to recognize the symptoms of weather-related ailments such as heat stroke and frostbite and how to do something about them before it's too late.

What to Carry

The first item on your list of things to carry is water, even if you're taking a short hike. It's all too easy to become dehydrated during a hike, especially in warm weather. So you'll need to drink plenty of water as you go, even if you don't feel particularly thirsty.

You can't count on finding drinkable water along your route, so you'll need to carry enough for your entire hike. If you're planning a short hike, you may be able to get away with one container or canteen. For longer hikes, try filling three or four containers so that you can distribute the weight evenly in your pack.

The next item on the list is food. Hiking takes a lot of energy—at least 300 calories an hour (more if you're hiking at a brisk pace or on rugged or uphill terrain). Even if you eat an extra large breakfast before you begin, you're likely to get hungry on the trail.

Because you'll probably have to carry all the food you'll need along the trail, try to choose foods that are nourishing yet low in weight and bulk—and easy to prepare in advance. Particularly in hot weather, avoid bringing perishable foods such as milk products and raw meat, which can spoil easily. Sandwiches and snacks of nuts, dried fruits, and dry cereal are favorite choices. They'll provide you with the carbohydrates you need for energy. A variety of dehydrated foods are also available, but these require water to make them edible.

An essential item to carry is a small first aid kit. At the very least, this kit should contain bandages or sterile pads and tape, antiseptic, and aspirin or another painkiller. In addition, you may want to carry a pocket knife or small pair of scissors, matches, a small flashlight, and a good sunscreen. You may also want to bring a compass along. If you have a map of the area, be sure to keep it in a handy spot as you walk.

To carry all these items, you'll need a pack. Which type you choose depends on the length of the hikes you intend to take. If you plan on taking short hikes, a fanny pack or day pack should be large enough. If you go on overnight hikes, however, you'll need a backpack that's roomier.

Packs come in a variety of models, sizes, materials, and colors. Some have internal frames, others have external frames. To find a pack that's right for you, visit a sporting goods store that has knowledgeable salespeople. Discuss with them the type of hiking you'll be doing and the amount of money you're willing to spend. They should be able to help you choose a suitable pack.

Be sure, however, to try the pack on before you purchase it. You'll be the one carrying it around, so you'll want it to feel comfortable. The pack should conform to your back. It should also have adjustable, padded shoulder straps and an adjustable waist belt that will allow you to distribute the weight of the pack to your hips as well as your shoulders.

Once you've taken several day hikes, you may want to try an overnight hiking or backpacking trip. For these trips, you'll need to carry more supplies, including extra food and water, a sleeping bag, a powerful flashlight, a change of clothes, and perhaps even a tent and a small camping stove. This collection of necessities can add up to a heavy load.

Government researchers have found that carrying more than 25 pounds of weight for long periods can do more harm than good, however, by straining the shoulders, back, and knees. This research grew out of complaints from soldiers who had to carry heavy packs during long marches. So it may be best to limit the load you carry on a hiking trip to 25 pounds, if it's at all possible—and even less if you are a woman. To cut down on weight, try choosing nourishing foods that don't need to be cooked, so you won't have to bring a stove. If you're purchasing a sleeping bag or tent, choose lightweight models. And when you pack, stick to the essentials.

Safety

Part of the challenge and pleasure of hiking is the chance it gives you to explore wild areas and experience the wonders of nature. Even if you're hiking a trail for the second time around, you'll probably discover sights and sounds that you missed the first time. Each hike offers you new opportunities and new experiences. But you can prevent some unpleasant surprises by taking a few precautions on the trail.

As a general safety precaution, it's best for all but the most experienced hikers to walk with a companion, especially on long treks. Before you venture out, its also wise to let someone at home know where you're going, which trail you intend to follow, and when you intend to return.

When you're on the trail, avoid drinking water directly from springs, streams, or lakes. No matter how clean and clear it looks, the water may be contaminated with a host of parasites and bacteria introduced by people or animals upstream from where you are. Boiling the water for at least one minute may help destroy some of these organisms. Portable water treatment kits are also available to help you purify water in an emergency. However, the best way to avoid illness from contaminated water is to carry safe drinking water with you on your hike.

Poisonous plants are another trailside hazard. To guard against getting rashes from poison ivy, poison oak, and poison sumac, wear clothing that covers as much exposed skin as possible, particularly on the feet and legs. Wear long pants, socks, and shoes or boots. When you return home from a hike, remove your hiking outfit and toss it in the washing machine. If you do develop a rash from one of these plants, try applying an over-the-counter remedy, such as calamine lotion, to relieve itching.

If you're going on an overnight trip in the wilderness, you can protect your food—and yourself—from wild animals by stringing your food up at night. Place all food and snacks, as well as toothpaste, lotion, and other pleasant-smelling items in a corded bag or your pack. Then string the bundle up high between two trees.

If you'll be hiking in an area that isn't off-limits to hunters, be sure to wear something bright, especially during hunting season. Otherwise, you might be mistaken for prey. Orange caps are very popular for this purpose, and they are available in a variety of materials, including ones that are waterproof and breathable.

Finally, before you head out, be sure to read Chapter 11 to find out how you can prevent conditions like heatstroke, frostbite, and dehydration while you're on the trail.

Great American Trails

There are all kinds of short-distance and long-distance hiking goals you may want to try to reach some day. The United States has an abundance of trails that can challenge your hiking skills. Some of the great trails include the Potomac Heritage Trail, the Daniel Boone

Trail, the Lewis and Clark Trail, the Mormon Pioneer Trail, the Oregon Trail, the Pacific Crest Trail, and the Continental Divide Trail.

One trail that has captured the hearts of hikers young and old for years is the Appalachian Trail. Hiking it will give you a sense of history as well as a real sense of accomplishment. Stretching from Maine to Georgia, the Appalachian Trail was originally a path used by migrating American Indians. It was this nation's first "interstate" and after the Revolution was maintained by the individual states through which it cut its swath. As vigorous a walk as it may seem to be, it has been conquered by a tremendous number of avid walkers.

Another great American trail is the Florida Trail, which acquaints walkers with Florida's wild side. The trail, which is still being blazed, is about 1,000 miles long already and will be over 1,300 miles long when it is completed. It stretches from the Big Cypress Swamp in the southwest part of the state (near Naples), through Wekiva Springs and Ocala National Forest in the center of the state, to Blackwater State Forest in the northwest portion of the state (near Pensacola). For information on the Florida Trail Association, which maintains the trail, see the Appendix.

Chapter 9

STRETCHES AND EXERCISES

The one exercise that will provide complete fitness for all parts of the body has not been devised. All exercises have their shortcomings. Swimmers and cyclists, unless they do specific exercises in addition to swimming and cycling, may have poor abdominal strength. People who practice yoga may lack cardiovascular strength. Walkers are no exception. Walking does not preserve flexibility, which is essential to preventing injury. It also doesn't do much for upper body strength. So in this chapter, we'll show you how to lower your risk of injury and round out your walking program.

Flexibility

Walking will not help you maintain or improve your flexibility (although it will enable arthritics to keep their affected joints flexible). Indeed, one complaint often heard from walkers is that before they began their walking program they could touch their toes, but after six months of walking they can't. The reason is that walking causes the muscles in the back of the legs to contract. Repeated contractions shorten these muscles, tendons, and ligaments.

Unless you do something to remedy it, this lack of flexibility can be a serious problem. It can set you up for a variety of painful injuries. These injuries can sideline you and deprive you of the health and fitness benefits of walking.

To maintain your flexibility and ward off injury, you need to stretch your muscles before you put them to work. Stretching, both before and after your workouts, is absolutely essential to your walking program. If you skip stretching to save time, you'll probably end up losing time in the end as you wait for your sore and injured muscles to heal.

Upper Body Strength

Walking—though good for cardiovascular fitness, weight control, and attractive legs—does little for the muscles of the upper body. While it will help you lose weight without losing desirable lean body tissue, it really won't build huge biceps or greatly strengthen your arms, neck, shoulders, and abdomen.

You don't have to give up on walking just because of this shortcoming, however. There are several things you can do to round out your walking program and provide your upper body with a workout. Using weights as you walk (see Chapter 7) is one solution. On the other hand, you can visit a local gymnasium or health club and use weights or weight machines to strengthen muscles throughout your body.

In addition to weight training, you can incorporate simple strengthening exercises into your walking program. These exercises don't require expensive equipment or loads of spare time. They can even be sandwiched between your walks and your stretches.

Stretching and Strengthening

On the following pages, you'll find a series of stretches that you can perform before and after each of your walking workouts. Before you begin stretching, warm up your muscles by walking slowly for a few minutes (you may try walking slowly in or around your home). Then stop walking and begin the stretches. They will loosen up your muscles and allow you to move more freely as you walk. They will also help prevent muscle soreness and injury.

End your walks with a cool-down period of slow walking followed by more stretching. By this time, your muscles will be loose, so you'll be able to stretch them further. By stretching after your walks, as well as before, you'll be able to improve your flexibility.

When you stretch, use a slow, smooth movement. Avoid bouncing, since this will cause the muscles to tighten. Stretch as far as you can, but don't stretch to the point of pain.

At the end of this chapter, you'll find several exercises that will help you strengthen your muscles, especially those in the upper part of your body. Try doing two or three of these exercises after your warm-up stretches, but before your walk. Then do two or three more before your cool-down stretches. Start out with 5 repetitions of each exercise and gradually build up to 30 or more "reps."

STRETCHES

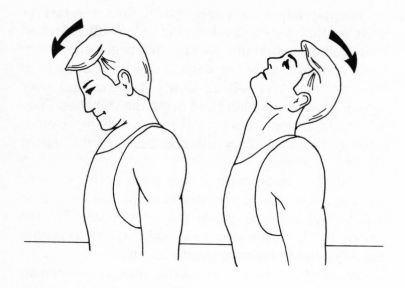

Head Flexor. Stand up straight with your arms at your sides. Slowly lower your chin to your chest, drawing your chin as far down as possible. Then slowly raise your chin and tilt your head backward as far as possible to complete one stretch. Repeat this stretch three times.

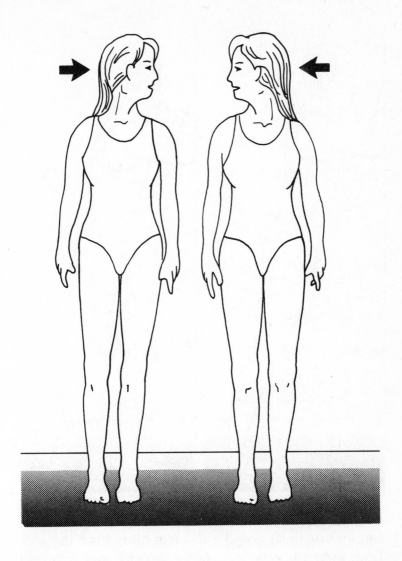

Neck Turns. Stand up straight with your arms at your sides. Turn your head slowly to the left and look over your left shoulder. Then turn your head slowly to the right and look over your right shoulder to complete one stretch. Repeat this stretch three times.

Calf Stretch. Face a wall (or anything sturdy that you can lean against). Stand a few feet away from the wall. Lean forward, with your body straight, and rest your forearms against the wall. Bend your right knee and move it closer to the wall. Keep your left leg straight. Be sure both heels remain on the ground. Keep your toes pointed straight ahead. Hold for 15 seconds. Repeat using the opposite leg to complete one stretch. Perform this stretch two times.

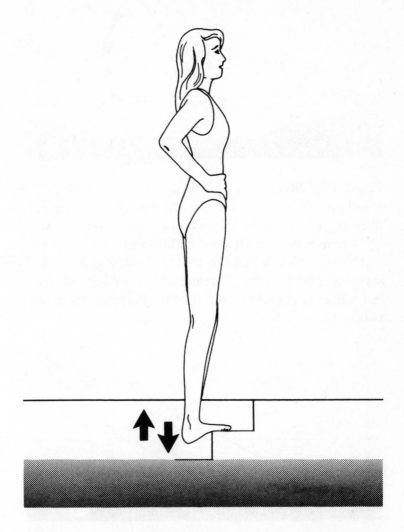

Raises. Stand straight with the balls and toes of your feet on the edge of a step. Your heels should not be supported by the step. Slowly lower your heels and hold for 15 seconds. Then slowly raise your heels and rise up on your toes. Hold for 15 seconds to complete one stretch. Perform this stretch two times.

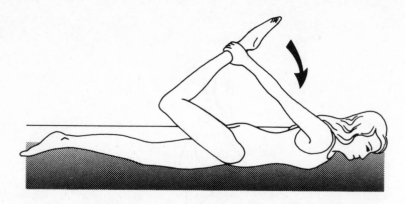

Front Leg Stretch. Lie face down on the ground or stand straight. (If you choose the upright position, you may need to stand near a wall or chair to steady yourself.) Reach back with your right hand and grasp your right ankle. Slowly pull the ankle to your hip, hold for 15 seconds, and release. Repeat using your left hand and left ankle to complete one stretch. Perform this stretch two or three times.

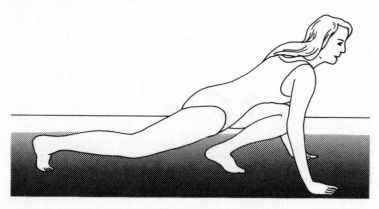

Sprinter. Assume a squatting position and place your hands on the floor in front of your feet. Extend one leg backward as far as possible. Hold for 15 seconds and release. Repeat using the other leg to complete one stretch. Perform this stretch two times.

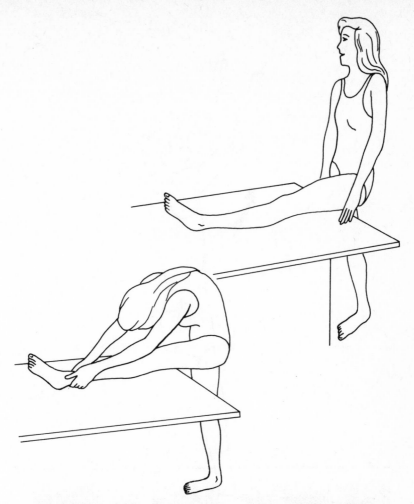

Standing Leg Stretch. Find a sturdy chair or table approximately three feet in height. Place one of your legs on the table so that the kneecap is facing straight up and the leg is parallel to the ground. Slowly lean forward and extend your fingertips toward the toes of the outstretched leg. Eventually you should be able to bring your forehead to your knee. Hold for several seconds and release. Repeat with the other leg to complete one stretch. Perform this stretch once.

*If you find this stretch too difficult, skip it and continue with the remaining stretches.

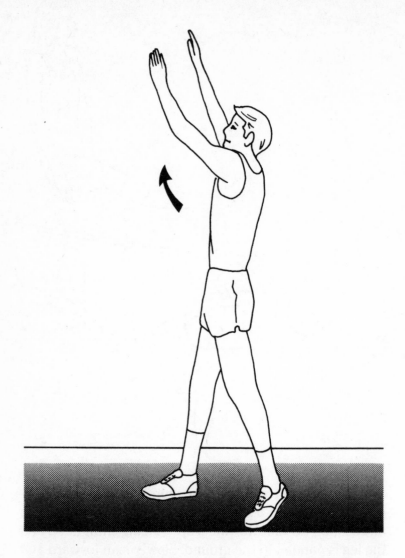

Parallel Arm Swings. Stand straight with your feet shoulder-width apart and your arms relaxed at your sides. Slowly swing both arms together to the right and upward as high as possible (this motion resembles a golf swing). Hold for five seconds and release. Then slowly swing both arms to the left and upward. Hold for five seconds to complete one stretch. Perform this stretch two times.

Shoulder Stretch. Lay your forearms on top of your head and grasp your right elbow with your left hand. Slowly pull the elbow behind your head. Don't force it. Hold this position for 15 seconds, then switch arms and do it again to complete 1 stretch. Perform this stretch one or two times.

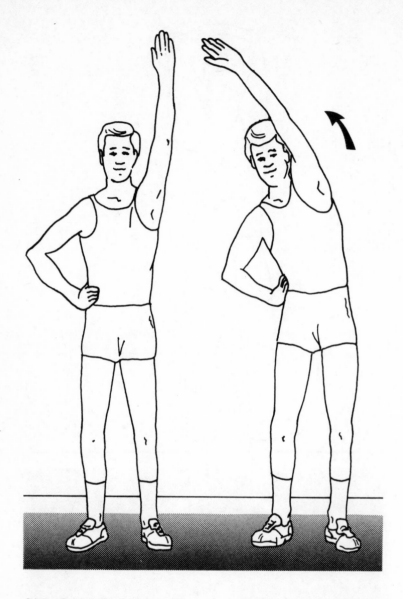

Side Stretch. Stand with your feet shoulder-width apart and your legs straight. Place your right hand on your right hip and extend your left arm above your head. Slowly bend to the right. Hold this position for 15 seconds, then repeat on the other side to complete one stretch. Perform this stretch three to five times.

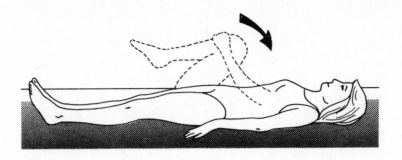

Lower Back Stretch. Lie on your back with your legs extended. Lift and bend one leg, grasp it at the knee, and slowly pull the knee to your chest. Keep the opposite leg straight. Hold for 15 seconds and release. Repeat with opposite leg to complete one stretch. Perform this stretch three to five times.

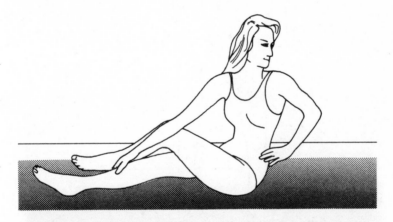

Spinal Stretch. Sit on the floor with your legs straight out in front of you. Keep your right leg straight and place your left foot on the other side of your right knee. Slowly and gently twist your body to the left. Place your right elbow against the outer side of your left knee and, with your right hand, grasp your right leg near the knee. Hold for 15 seconds and release. Repeat on the other side to complete one stretch. Perform this stretch one time.

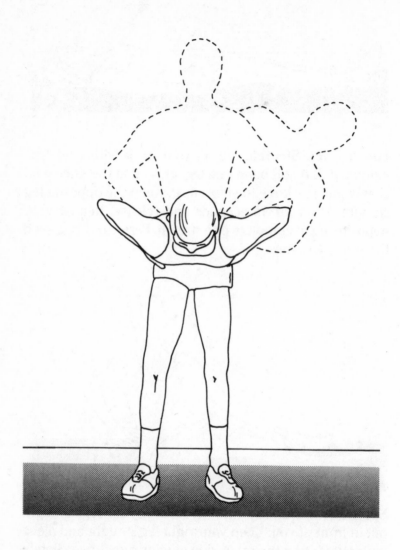

Abdominal Churn. Stand straight with your hands on your hips. Slowly bend sideways to the left, then rotate your upper body forward, then to the right, and finally to the upright position. Repeat in the reverse direction to complete one stretch. Perform this stretch three times.

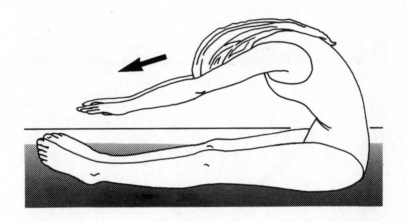

Sitting Toe Touches. Sit on the floor with your legs extended in front of you and your feet together. Slowly reach for your toes, bringing your forehead as close to your knees as possible. Hold for 15 seconds and release. Perform this stretch one time.

EXERCISES FOR STRENGTH

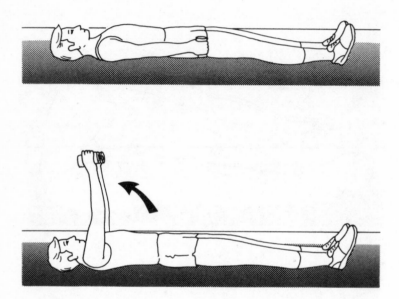

Arm Arc. For this exercise, you'll need small weights (books or unopened cans of food make good weights). Lie on your back with weights in your hands and your arms at your sides. Raise your arms upward in an arc to shoulder height, then return to the starting position to complete one repetition.

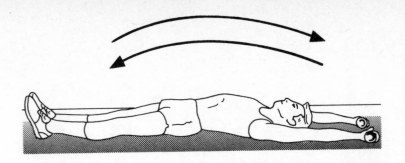

Arms Over. Lie on your back, arms at your sides, with weights in your hands. Raise the weights up and over your head, reaching as far back as possible. Return to the starting position to complete one repetition.

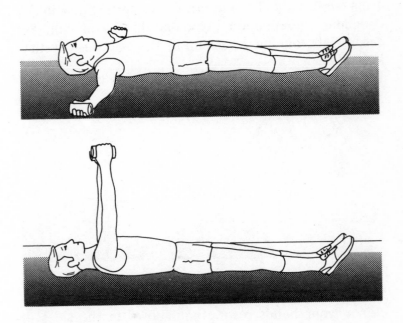

Right Angles. Lie on your back with weights in your hands and your arms on the ground at right angles to your body. Raise your arms so that they point straight up, pulling in your abdomen at the same time. Return to the starting position to complete one repetition.

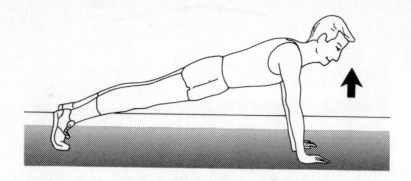

Regular Push-up. Lie face-down with your feet together and your hands palm-down beneath your shoulders. Keeping your body straight, push your entire body, except for your hands and feet, off the floor until your arms are straight. Then return to the starting position to complete one repetition. If you find this too difficult, you can use the modified push-up or the wall push-up that follow.

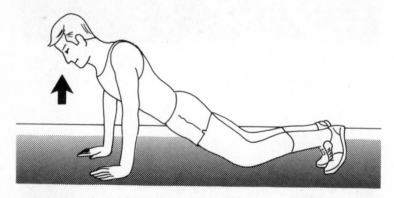

Modified Push-up. Lie face-down with your feet together, your hands resting palm-down to the sides of your shoulders, and your fingers pointed forward. Lift your body from the knees up by straightening your arms; and keep your back straight. Return to the starting position to complete one repetition. Note that the farther apart you place your hands, the more you'll develop your chest muscles.

Wall Push-up. Stand about three to four feet away from a wall. Place your hands palm-down on the wall at shoulder height. Keeping your body straight, slowly bend your arms until you can touch your chin to the wall. Return to the starting position to complete one repetition. This is a good strengthening exercise for the elderly or less fit.

Trunk Twister. Stand with your hands clasped behind your neck and your elbows drawn back. As you walk in place, raise your right knee as high as possible and turn your body to the right so that your left elbow briefly touches your right knee. When your right foot hits the floor, raise your left knee as high as possible and turn your body to the left so that your right elbow touches your left knee. This completes one repetition.

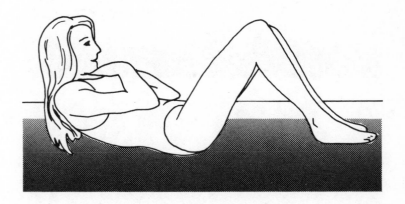

Head and Shoulder Curl. Lie on your back with your knees bent, your feet on the floor, and your arms crossed on your chest. (If you prefer, you may clasp your hands behind your head or place your arms at your sides.) Tighten your abdominal muscles and curl your head and shoulders up off the floor. Do not lift your back off the floor. Return to the starting position to complete one repetition.

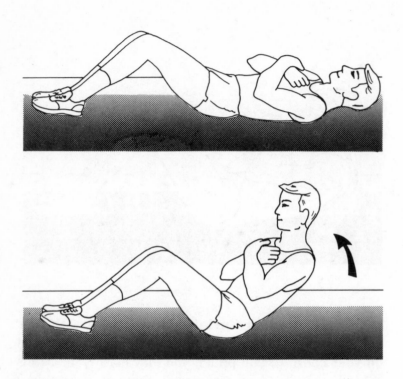

Sit-up. Lie on your back with your knees bent and your arms across your chest. (If you prefer, you may place your arms at your sides, extend your arms over your head, or clasp your hands behind your head.) Curl your body up into a sitting position by first drawing your chin toward your chest, then lifting your upper body off the floor. Keep your back rounded throughout the movement. Sit up as far as possible, then return to the starting position to complete one repetition.

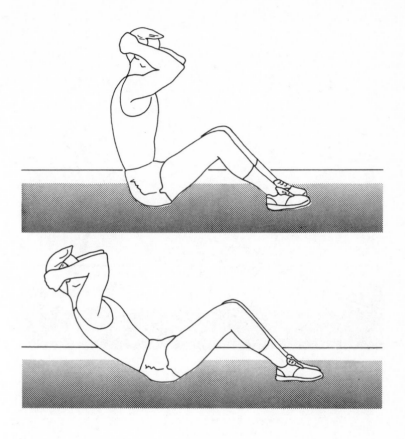

Curl-down. Start from a sitting position with your knees bent and your hands clasped behind your head. Lower your upper body halfway to the ground, so that it forms a 45 degree angle with the ground. Keep your back rounded throughout the movement. Hold that position for a few seconds and return to the upright position to complete one repetition.

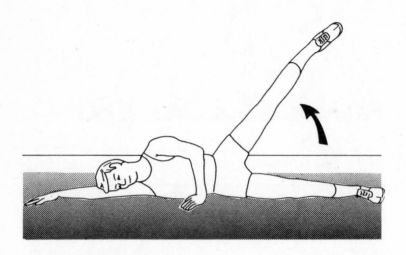

Single Leg Raises. Lie on your right side with your right arm extended above your head (palm against the floor) and your head resting on your extended arm. Place your left hand on the floor in front of you for stability. Raise your left leg to at least a 45 degree angle. Lower your leg to the starting position to complete one repetition. Do several repetitions then turn over and do the exercise on your other side.

Swing and Bounce. Stand with your feet shoulder-width apart and your knees bent at 45 degree angles. Your body should lean forward and your arms should hang relaxed. Swing one arm forward as the other one swings back. Continue by reversing the position of your arms with an easy swinging motion. As you continue this motion, bend your knees more and then straighten them. Try to coordinate your arm swings with your knee bends. Continue this movement for a few minutes.

Chapter 10

COPING
WITH
PAIN

W e've said repeatedly that a well-designed walking program should enable you to enjoy the benefits of aerobic training without pain. However, no matter how carefully you follow the CONSUMER GUIDE® Walking Program, you'll probably experience a few little aches and pains—simply because you'll be asking your body to do things that it might not have done for years.

We have included this chapter on coping with pain because we don't want a few minor physical discomforts to discourage you from walking. Here we'll explain the types of pain or discomfort you may encounter and what to do about them. As you continue to walk, you will undoubtedly gather your own little private collection of twinges and throbs—"body noises" that may be completely new to you. You are the best judge of what they mean, so pay attention to them. Pain is one way your body has of communicating with you. It takes practice to decode the messages—but it's worth it. A few aches and pains are okay; just listen to your body. Most of the time, your pain will be caused by improper walking technique; improper shoes or socks; walking surfaces that are too hard; or too much walking, too soon. If you have any doubts, however, check with your doctor.

Often the solution to the pain-causing problem is so simple that you miss it. For instance, several members of a walking class once complained of continual pain in their left knees. They tried wearing different shoes and taping their knees; nothing seemed to help. Yet the source of the problem turned out to be quite simple. These exercisers had been walking on a track that was banked (in other words, it tilted upward from the inside edge). The slant of the track had gradually created an imbalance in their walking style and a strain on their left knees, which were always on the down side of the incline. So their instructor asked them to change the direction of their walks every day or two. That way, the same leg wouldn't always be on the down side of the track. This simple solution worked like magic. Their pain disappeared almost immediately.

Solutions to pain puzzlers aren't always this simple, but this case shows how the solution can often be found by a little self-analysis. Everyone will experience some discomfort. That's one reason you'll want to ask other walkers what they have experienced. Many problems are widespread, and most of the solutions rely on plain common sense.

The ironic thing about aerobic exercises is that those organs we mainly want to exercise for the aerobic training effect—the heart and lungs—aren't the chief source of most of our discomfort. Instead, it's the feet, ankles, and legs—which have to work so hard to exercise the heart and lungs—that cause the most trouble.

To help prevent injuries and keep your walking pain to a minimum, you should do three things: Take good care of your feet; strengthen the muscles in your feet, legs, and abdomen; and develop flexibility throughout your body.

Conditioning of the muscles in your lower body will take place naturally and automatically as you walk. But you can help it along by supplementing your walking with calisthenics or other activities that will help you build strength. To maintain and develop flexibility, however, you'll need to include plenty of stretches in your walking routine (see Chapter 9).

From the Ground Up

What follows is a brisk summary of the types of aches and pains that walkers sometimes feel. We'll begin at the bottom, discussing minor ailments of the feet, then move on up until we reach the chest, where pain or discomfort can be especially worrisome because it can signal heart trouble.

Prior to discussing the feet, however, it's important to note that people suffering from diabetes or circulatory problems should consult their doctor before embarking on a walking program. These individuals are particularly prone to ailments of the feet, and the consequences of even a minor cut or bruise can be severe.

The toes. If you begin a walking program wearing shoes that are long on fashion and short on comfort, your toes will almost certainly let you know what a mistake you've made. Most toe discomfort results from poorly fitting shoes. Finding shoes that fit, however, is a lot more complicated than simply getting, say, a "nine medium" because you measured that size at a fitting years ago.

The length, width, and shape of your feet can—and do—change. With age, the ball of the foot tends to widen and the toes tend to spread. When women bear children, their feet may get longer and wider. Therefore, it is a good idea to have your feet measured again each time you shop for shoes.

The size marked on a shoe doesn't really tell you whether it will fit your foot. Some manufacturers' sizes run large, while others run small. Even among shoes from the same manufacturer, one style may run large, while another runs small. The shape of your foot finally determines the shoe that you should choose for maximum comfort. Select a design that matches the general shape of your foot as closely as possible. One way to do this is to trace your feet on a sheet of paper. Then, when you go to the store, compare your tracing to the bottoms of various shoes.

When you try on a pair of walking shoes, be sure they fit well in the toe area. One of your feet is probably larger than the other, and that bigger foot is the one you'll want to fit. Ideally, there will be a half-inch space between the end of the longest toe of your bigger foot and the inside end of the shoe. And each shoe's "toe box," the part of the shoe that cradles the toes, should be high, long, and wide enough to accommodate your toes comfortably. (See Chapter 15 for more information on walking shoes.)

Corns. Corns are small, round mounds of dead skin caused by friction. Hard corns, the most common type, are dry and found most often on the outside of the smallest toe or on top of the other toes; soft corns are moist and usually appear between the toes.

In some cases, you can relieve corns by opting for shoes with softer uppers and toe boxes that are wider, longer, and higher. Cushioned pads or insoles can also offer relief by shifting pressure away from corns. If these efforts do not provide relief, see a podiatrist. Never attempt to remove a corn yourself.

Ingrown toenails. Few things are more aggravating to a walker than ingrown toenails. Ingrown toenails are nails, usually of the big toe, that curve inward along the edges, causing pain, redness, swelling, and even bacterial infection. To prevent them, you need to keep your toenails trimmed. However, be careful not to taper the nails or trim them too short in the corners, since this can set the stage for ingrown toenails. Instead, trim the toenails straight across with a nail clipper.

Ingrown toenails can be aggravated by toe boxes that are too tight, so switching to a shoe with a wider toe box may help to relieve discomfort. Soaking the affected toe in warm, soapy water may also provide temporary relief. If the area around the ingrown toenail is severely swollen and painful, however, see your podiatrist. Never try to remove an ingrown toenail yourself.

Bunions. A bunion is a deformity of the big toe joint in which the joint juts outward and the big toe angles inward toward the other toes. Although the tendency to develop this condition can be inherited, wearing pointy, high-heeled shoes or shoes that are too tight in the toe area can aggravate it. As the joint becomes more inflamed, the bunion grows and becomes more swollen, tender, and painful.

A podiatrist may begin treatment by having you wear wider shoes and by prescribing a custom-made shoe insert called an orthotic (also known as an orthosis). The orthotic is made to compensate for the abnormality in the shape of the foot and to shift weight away from the problem area.

An orthotic may make living with a bunion easier. However, if the bunion is already very large and painful, and if it interferes with walking, then surgery is frequently the only way to relieve the problem. In bunion surgery, the toe joint is realigned and excess bone may be removed.

Hammertoes. Hammertoe is a deformity in which a toe (or toes) hooks downward like a claw. Hammertoes often run in families. High heels or shoes that fit too tightly in the toe area, however, are common culprits in causing pain. If the toe is severely hooked and painful, and interferes with walking, then surgery may be necessary to straighten it out.

Neuromas. A neuroma is an abnormal collection of nerves that becomes irritated and inflamed. Neuromas occur between the bases of two toes, usually the third and fourth ones. Again, tight-fitting shoes can aggravate this condition. Neuromas can cause stabbing pain or a numb sensation. Soaking in warm water may help relieve the discomfort. Your doctor may prescribe an arch support or a special pad that can be placed inside your shoe to spread the nerve-pinching toes apart. Surgery to remove the neuroma is the last resort.

Metatarsal stress fractures. The metatarsals are the long bones in your feet that are attached to the base of your toes. From the stress of walking, the metatarsals can develop fractures so small that they may not be visible on an X ray. Often, they don't have to be splinted or put into a cast; they simply heal by themselves. But healing takes time, sometimes a month or two, and you'll probably have to suspend your walking program until this healing process is complete.

Blisters. These pockets of clear fluid or blood are common ailments. Regardless of the type of shoe worn and the protective measures taken, foot blisters continue to pose a problem for many people. They become a major problem only when they are severe enough to affect the quantity and quality of walking or when they become infected.

Foot blisters are caused by friction. The best way to prevent blisters is to prevent the friction that causes them. Here are some recommendations for doing that:

1. Buy high-quality shoes and make sure they fit properly.

2. Take good care of your shoes. Don't allow them to get brittle and stiff.

3. Break in new shoes before walking very far. A good idea is first to wear the shoes around the house for a few minutes each day. As they begin to soften, wear them for walking short distances. Once they're broken in, you can wear them for longer distances. Try buying new shoes before your old ones wear out completely, so you won't be tempted to rush the break-in process.

4. Wear socks or stockings to help prevent blisters. The socks should be clean and should fit snugly. If they are too big, they can bunch up and cause friction. Ideally, the socks should not have seams in the foot area.

When a blister does develop, you can prevent infection by keeping the area clean. Do not puncture blisters. Leave them alone; bit by bit, they'll drain internally. If a blister ruptures, do not remove the skin; it serves as a protective covering. After a gentle cleaning with soap and water, place a pad of gauze over the open blister. Resting the foot will aid healing. Consult your doctor or podiatrist at the first sign of infection, such as redness or pus. If you are diabetic or have circulatory problems, consult your doctor at the first sign of a blister, no matter how small.

Calluses. A callus is a thickening of the skin at places of pressure or friction (like the soles of the feet). A moderate amount of callus formation is normal; it's one way the foot protects itself. But when thick, hard calluses form, they can be painful. To help relieve pain, try switching to a shoe with softer uppers and a roomier toe box. Cushioned pads or insoles, and orthotics, can help. A simple scraping of the calluses by a podiatrist can also yield dramatic pain relief. Never try cutting calluses off yourself.

Walker's heel. This is a term some people use to describe a group of heel problems that include bone bruises and heel spurs. The syndrome usually starts with pain at the base of the heel—called plantar fasciitis, which involves inflammation of the tissues that attach to the bottom of the heel bone. Bone spurs are painful bony growths on the bone itself. These ailments may be worsened by walking on a hard surface, stepping on sharp objects, or walking in poorly designed shoes. These conditions don't lend themselves to a quick cure. Rest is good for them, but not always desirable for the person who wants to maintain his or her aerobic conditioning.

As far as treatment is concerned, a heel "donut" is often helpful. This is nothing more than a foam pad with a hole cut in it. The foam pad is placed over the bone spur, with the sensitive spot protruding through the hole. The pad is then taped to your foot. Many people have had excellent success with this. Other modes of treatment include strapping the foot with an athletic bandage or switching to a shoe that has a springy rubber sole and a slightly higher heel (this helps shift the pressure of walking from the heel to the ball of the foot). Also useful for pain relief are warm soaks. If these measures don't work for you, see a podiatrist.

Achilles tendon injuries. The Achilles tendon is the thick tendon at the back of the leg that connects the heel and foot to the back of the calf muscles. It controls the hinge-like action of the ankle with every walking step and therefore does a lot of work during a walk.

Experts in sports medicine have identified three types of problems with the Achilles tendon. The first is tendonitis, which is an inflammation of the tendon. The second is a partial rupture, which is a tearing of some of the tendon fibers. The third is a complete rupture, or a complete break, of the tendon itself. The last two are not common to walkers, because walking seldom puts enough stress on the tendon to actually tear it.

Tendonitis can be caused by a sudden change in routine, such as wearing different shoes, walking on grass and then switching to cinders, or abruptly changing from one type of exercise training to another. Symptoms of tendonitis are pain and stiffness an hour or so following activity, tenderness, and slight swelling. Tendonitis makes walking very difficult and painful.

Tendons also become inflamed when they are constricted by equipment. If you feel pain in your Achilles tendons, your walking shoes could be the culprits. The heels may be too low or too hard, the backs may be so tight that they strain or crowd the tendon, or the arch support in the shoes may not be supplying adequate support. So you may need to try a different pair of shoes.

The very act of walking often tightens these tendons even more. This is just one reason why stretching exercises are important to the walker. They limber up the tendons and counteract the tightening effects of walking.

Self-treatment of tendonitis is summarized by the acronym RICE—rest, ice, compression, elevation. If it hurts, stop the activity. Place ice or a cold compress on the affected area. Then wrap it in a flexible bandage (not too tight) and sit or lie down with your leg elevated. Remember, pain is a message that your body is sending to you. Don't ignore it.

To prevent Achilles tendonitis from developing, make sure that you do plenty of stretching in your warm-ups. Suggested stretching exercises include standing on the heels of the feet and drawing your toes up as far as possible or standing with your toes on a step and stretching your heels downward. Another good idea is to walk barefooted whenever possible—preferably indoors, so you won't have to worry about stepping on sharp objects.

Also avoid sudden and violent changes in routine, such as walking on a level surface and then abruptly switching to sharp inclines or walking short distances and then abruptly taking a long hike.

Choosing a walking shoe with a slightly higher heel or inserting a sponge pad in the heel section of your shoes can help prevent the pain of Achilles tendonitis and of heel spurs, according to Charles Gudas, D.P.M, professor of orthopedic surgery and rehabilitative medicine at the University of Chicago Medical Center. But note that this does not mean that high heels are good for you—just that a slightly higher heel on a walking shoe can be helpful for certain conditions.

Shin splints. Shin splints refers to pain on the front of the shin. If you have shin splints, you will feel pain in the lower leg when you put weight on your foot. You'll probably also find that your shin is tender to the touch. When you run your fingers along the shin, you may feel a roughened area along the bone.

Although the name implies damage to the shin bone, shin splints may actually be caused by a variety of problems, including a muscle imbalance; improper body mechanics while walking; a hairline fracture of one of the bones in the lower leg; a muscle spasm caused by swelling of the muscle in the front of the leg; an inflamed or torn tendon in the lower leg; or irritation of the membrane between the two bones of the lower leg.

You can help prevent shin splints by choosing footwear and walking surfaces carefully. Sturdy shoes with cushioned soles are a must. If possible, switch from a hard walking surface to a soft one. A golf course or local park offers the walker a chance to work out on grass, which is much softer than pavement or a track. You may also want to try putting a sponge heel pad in the heel section of your shoe to help absorb some of the stress from walking on harder surfaces. If you walk on a track, vary the direction of your walks. In other words, instead of always going clockwise, walk counterclockwise on alternate days so that you do not always place stress on the inside of the same leg as you go around the turns.

To prevent shin splints from occurring, it's also a good idea to condition the muscles in the front of the leg. Walking does a great deal to strengthen the muscles in the back of the leg, but it does less for those in the front. As a result, a muscle imbalance can occur. To compensate, you'll want to strengthen the muscles in the front. Flexing your foot up and down while wearing weights can help. If you don't have weights handy to strap onto your feet, sit with your legs dangling, feet not touching the floor, and have a friend hold your feet while you try to pull your toes up. Do this for three sets of ten each day.

The knee. The knee is a true hinge joint. The two main bones that come together at this joint are the thighbone and the shinbone. Usually, knee pains are associated with the kneecap—beneath it or along its sides. Sometimes the kneecap doesn't move smoothly against the lower end of the thighbone as it should, and the knee becomes increasingly irritated and swollen as you walk. If you have this problem, you may have to limit your walking. But first experiment with different walking methods. Many doctors think this problem may be caused or aggravated by the way your foot strikes the ground. If you walk indoors on a banked track in one direction for long distances, say 20 to 25 laps, your knees may be headed for trouble. Even subtle slopes such as that in a banked track can cause knee problems.

Many walkers and runners develop a painful affliction called runner's knee, in which the kneecap moves from side to side with each step. The reason is most often a foot that collapses inward during walking (or running). When the foot collapses, the lower leg rotates inward and the kneecap moves to the inside. Repeated foot strikes, in combination with this poor foot structure, will adversely affect the knee. Treatment usually consists of inserting orthotics in the shoes. It's also important for the walker to do leg exercises to strengthen and stretch the muscles on the front of the thighs.

Muscle cramps and spasms. A muscle cramp is an involuntary, powerful, and painful contraction of a muscle. The contraction may occur at any time—at rest as well as during activity. Cramps usually happen without warning. Occasionally, however, you may be able to feel one building up.

Among the causes of muscle cramps are the following: fatigue; cold; imbalance of salt, potassium, and water levels in the body; poor blood circulation to the muscles; a sharp blow; and overstretching of unconditioned muscles.

You may be able to reduce your odds of getting a muscle cramp by eating a well-balanced diet, by making sure you warm up properly before vigorous exercise, and by stopping activity before you become extremely tired.

Once a cramp does occur, you can usually stop it by gently stretching the affected muscle. For instance, to relieve a cramp in your calf muscle, get hold of the toes and ball of your foot and pull them toward your kneecap. It is also useful to knead the affected muscle firmly.

Usually, a sense of tightness or dull pain will follow. Applying heat or massaging the area may help relieve this discomfort. If you're plagued by frequent cramps, consult your doctor.

Sprains. Cramps and spasms are painful contractions of muscle tissue. In contrast, a sprain is a partial or complete rupture (tearing) of a muscle, tendon, or ligament, caused by overstretching. Small blood vessels in the area break and pain develops when the surrounding tissue swells up and stimulates sensitive nerve endings.

To help prevent ankle sprains, you need to watch where you're going. This means that even if you are the casual type and not too finicky about walking on a particular kind of surface, you should at least learn how to pick your way among the potholes and skillfully sidestep any debris in your path. If you aren't very good at that and manage to sprain your ankle, you'll have to suspend your walking program until it is healed. Again, RICE (rest, ice, compression, and elevation) will help bring down the swelling.

Muscle soreness and stiffness. Even people who have been serious walkers for years complain of regular soreness and stiffness. The pain may develop immediately after the activity or following some delay, usually 24 to 48 hours. Often the discomfort lasts for only a few days, although after periods of extremely intense exercise, it may last for a week. The most commonly affected muscles are the calves and front and back muscles of the thigh.

Medical authorities aren't certain what causes soreness and stiffness. The pain during and immediately after exercise is probably caused by waste products formed during exercise and left in the fluid that surrounds the cells within the muscles. When stiffness occurs approximately 24 to 48 hours after exercise, it may be the result of small muscle tears or localized contractions of the muscles.

It is practically impossible to completely avoid muscle soreness and stiffness. But you can reduce the intensity of the discomfort by planning your conditioning program so that you progress gradually, especially during the early stages. The slow, steady approach will allow the muscles of the body to adapt themselves to the stress placed upon them. If you become sore and stiff from physical activity, doing some additional light exercises or general activity will often provide temporary relief, though the pain will probably return when you stop. Including a cool-down period at the end of a workout will also help you avoid such undesirable aftereffects. Massage may also help.

Back pains. Don't fool around when you get back pains, especially if they are in the lower back. Lower-back pain can signal a slipped or damaged spinal disc. Obviously, back problems cannot be diagnosed on the walking path, but if you have a slipped disc, you'll know it—fast.

Some lower back pains result from exercising after years of relative inactivity. You will have to guess at the seriousness of these pains by the way you feel at the time; that is, how intense they are, how disabling they are, and so on. If you have any doubts, however, see your doctor.

There are, of course, several traditional explanations for back pain and discomfort. You've probably heard them already, but they're worth repeating. Improper sitting posture can lead to lower back problems. To sit slouched in a chair all day puts unnecessary tension on the back muscles. So you need to keep your back straight when you're seated. Furniture that is constructed without regard for body structure can also cause strain, fatigue, and muscle pain. If possible, select furniture that provides plenty of support for your back. (Some office furniture is designed specifically for this purpose.) Sitting for prolonged periods of time causes shortening of certain postural muscles, particularly the hamstrings in back of the thighs. If you sit all day at work, you must do stretching exercises regularly to keep your hamstring muscles at their proper length.

A mattress that is too soft or that sags in the middle is one of your back's worst enemies. No matter how you lie on this kind of mattress, your muscles are under constant tension all night long. It is no wonder that these muscles are sore in the morning. Many medical experts suggest the use of a board under the mattress to alleviate the condition. You might also consider purchasing an extra-firm mattress that will support your back as you sleep.

Often, however, the real problem is poor fitness—specifically, weak abdominal muscles. At the pelvis, the weight of the upper body is transferred to the lower limbs. The pelvis, or pelvic girdle, is balanced on the rounded heads of the thighbones. It is held in place by numerous muscles, including the abdominals, the hamstrings, the gluteals, and the hip flexors (for an illustration of these muscles, see page 22). An imbalance or weakness in these muscles can lead to pelvic misalignment, which usually causes the pelvis to tilt forward or backward.

If the abdominal muscles are weak, the top of the pelvis will drop and tilt forward. Forward tilt of the pelvis leads to lordosis, or sway back.

In addition to abdominal weakness, a lack of strength in the gluteals and hamstrings can lead to forward pelvic tilt. While the abdominals stabilize the pelvis by pulling upward on the front, the gluteals and hamstrings contribute to stabilizing by pulling down on the rear of the pelvis.

Exercises must be done to strengthen the abdominals and gluteals. Usually, walking is enough to do this for the gluteals. But the abdominal muscles must be conditioned in other ways, such as through weight training or calisthenics (see Chapter 9 for exercises you can do to strengthen your abdominal muscles).

If you have back trouble, or if you experience back pain when you walk, consult your doctor before beginning or continuing your walking program.

Side stitch. Side stitch goes by many names. It is called a pain in the side, a stitch in the side, side ache, or just plain stitch. Sometimes it frightens people because it happens near the chest area. There are as many explanations for the cause of side stitch as there are names to describe it. But there appear to be two basic causes.

The first is improper breathing. This causes spasms in the diaphragm. To reduce this problem, "belly breathing" is suggested. That is, when you inhale, push your abdomen out. When you exhale, pull in your abdomen. It's just the reverse of what you normally do.

The second cause is probably the most common. It's a stretching of the ligaments that attach themselves to the liver, pancreas, stomach, and intestines. These ligaments are put under stress when you walk vigorously. The bouncing action causes them to stretch, thereby causing pain.

One way to ease the discomfort of side stitch is simply to grip your side and push it in. There are some other things you can try, too. For instance, try not to eat a heavy meal within the three hours prior to the start of your walk. During the attack of side stitch, bend forward, inhale deeply, and push your belly out. If the pain is intolerable, lie flat on your back, raise your legs over your head, and support your hips. If that doesn't relieve the discomfort, see your doctor.

Chest Pain: How Serious Is It?

Any pain in the chest, no matter what its cause, can be troubling—especially if you've reached middle age, when the risk of heart disease rises. Such pain may have nothing to do with your heart. However, chest pain should never be ignored nor allowed to persist. Any chest pain or discomfort, no matter how minor, should be brought to the attention of your doctor.

We are warned so often about heart disease that the slightest twinge in the chest area can conjure up frightening visions of permanent disability, or even death, from heart disease. A seizure in the chest can be, and often is, caused by cardiovascular disease. But far more often it is caused by a simpler and less threatening ailment, such as heartburn or a strained muscle. In this section, we'll explain some of the possible causes of chest pain. This discussion is meant to be informative, but it should not be used as a substitute for a trip to the doctor.

Muscular causes. Chest pain or discomfort can be caused by a muscle spasm. A pulled pectoral (chest muscle) or a strained intracostal (side muscle) can cause a great deal of pain. A pulled muscle produces pain that is felt near the surface, and movements such as swinging the arm across the chest can initiate or worsen the pain. Bruised muscles and ligaments may cause pain during deep breathing and may be sensitive to the touch. Pressure during sleep from a hand, mattress button, or even a wrinkled sheet may aggravate bruised muscles. Pain associated with this kind of condition usually happens only during a certain motion or when pressure is applied to the area. Rest and time are usually the best treatments. Consult your doctor, however, to be sure.

Heartburn. The pain brought on by indigestion, or heartburn, is frequently confused with pain caused by heart trouble. But it has nothing to do with the heart. Acid from the stomach backs up into the esophageal tube, causing contractions of the circular muscle of the esophagus. Milk or antacids may provide temporary relief, but a simple, well-balanced diet is the best prevention. Heartburn is often confused with heart disease. If you can attribute the pain to a specific food, your worries may be over. To be sure, however, see your doctor.

Angina pectoris. This type of chest pain or discomfort can occur when you're at rest, but it often develops during exercise, when emotion is high, or after a heavy meal. It is the result of a temporary failure of the coronary arteries to deliver enough oxygenated blood to the heart muscle. Such a failure is usually the result of obstructions to coronary circulation.

Angina usually isn't a sharp pain; it is usually a sensation of heaviness, as if the chest were being squeezed or crushed. The discomfort often spreads to the left shoulder, arm, or hand, where it may be felt as numbness. It may also be felt in the neck, jaw, and teeth. Pain or discomfort may occur minutes, days, weeks, months, or even years apart.

Angina is a warning sign. Your heart is telling you to stop. Almost anyone can experience angina—people who have recovered from a heart attack, those who are going to have a heart attack, and even some who will never have a heart attack. The problem is that the heart is not getting enough blood, and therefore enough oxygen. If you experience any pain or discomfort resembling angina, report it to your doctor immediately. Your doctor will probably want you to be very specific about where and when the discomfort occurs so he or she can more fully understand your condition.

The other pains or discomfort associated with heart disease are varied, yet similar to angina. They may be sharp, mild, or numbing. If you experience any of these pains, particularly a heavy sensation in the chest or a pain that radiates up the neck or down the arm, contact your doctor immediately.

The following symptoms may signal a heart attack: an extreme heaviness in the center of your chest; an extreme tightness, like a clenched fist inside the center of your chest; or a feeling of stuffiness (something like indigestion) high in your stomach or low in your throat. Whenever you have a symptom that resembles any one of these, stop walking and get to your doctor.

You may have gone through a stress electrocardiogram before you started a walking program and passed it with flying colors. If so, your chances of experiencing these symptoms are relatively small. But don't become cocky. A stress electrocardiogram, like most tests, is not 100 percent reliable. In the final analysis, your body, not somebody else's electronic equipment, has the final word. So listen to it.

Chapter 11

WALK, WEATHER OR NOT

Some days, the weather's going to be ideal for walking—very light breeze, temperature around 60 degrees, not a cloud in sight. What do you do, however, when the snow starts to fall, a gale threatens to blow you off the path, or the heat makes you feel as if your shoes will melt? It may not sound too appealing to you now, but you can walk in all but the worst weather. If you make walking as much a part of your routine as eating or sleeping, you'll probably find yourself walking through rain, snow, and sleet—and enjoying every minute of it.

The secret to all-weather walking is to be prepared—with appropriate clothing and gear and the knowledge of when to back off. Temperature extremes can be more than uncomfortable; they can be dangerous and even fatal if you don't prepare yourself adequately. But with good preparation, you can keep on walking outdoors under all but the most extreme weather conditions.

Too Darn Hot

No matter how fit you are, you need to be careful when you walk in hot weather—especially if the humidity is high. Even experienced athletes can fall victim to serious heat-related ailments if they don't take special precautions. In some instances, you may simply have to stop walking outdoors and move your walking program inside, into an air-conditioned track, gym, or mall (see Chapter 12 on where to walk).

Your body has a built-in cooling system that helps it to maintain a proper temperature (usually 98.6 degrees Fahrenheit) when you're in a hot environment. Sweat plays a major role in this cooling system. The evaporation of sweat from the surface of your skin causes cooling. In addition, the blood vessels in your skin dilate (expand) to let more blood flow through them. (That's why you get a flushed look when you're working hard.) As your blood circulates through the innermost region of your body, known as the body core, it heats up. When it reaches the blood vessels in the skin, the heat radiates outward.

This natural "air-conditioning" system isn't foolproof, however. If you don't replace the water that you lose through sweat, you can become dehydrated and your blood volume can decrease. Without adequate water, your sweating mechanism can't work effectively. In the extreme case, this mechanism can shut down completely.

High humidity coupled with warm temperatures can also greatly hamper your body's ability to stay cool. When it's humid, there's already so much moisture in the air that your sweat can't evaporate as quickly. (On the other hand, a breeze can help your body maintain proper temperature by aiding in the evaporation of sweat.) As a result, your body loses water as it pumps out sweat, yet your body temperature continues to rise.

Another important factor in how well your body deals with heat is *acclimatization*. Your body needs anywhere from four days to two weeks to make physiological adjustments that allow it to cope with extreme heat. As the body becomes acclimatized, it lowers its threshold for sweating—in other words, it switches on the sweating mechanism before body temperature rises too high. In addition, it produces more sweat and distributes the sweat more effectively over the skin surface to allow cooling. The body also directs more blood toward the surface of the skin so that heat from deep within the body core can radiate out of the body. If the body hasn't had time to make these adjustments, however, it may not be able to handle heat effectively.

If you overdo it in the heat, you can develop a series of problems. There are three major types of heat illness: heat cramps, heat exhaustion, and heatstroke. Heat cramps are the least serious and heatstroke the most threatening. Their symptoms overlap, however, and if proper measures aren't taken at the first sign of heat injury, heat illness can progress to its most severe form.

Heat cramps are painful muscle spasms that occur during or after intense exercise. They usually occur in the muscles that are being exercised and appear to be caused by the loss of water and salt through sweat. The body temperature is usually not elevated. Rest and replacement of water and salt can help relieve heat cramps.

Heat exhaustion, also called heat prostration, is a common heat-related illness that occurs most often in people who are not acclimatized to hot weather. It appears to be caused by the body's ineffective adjustment of the circulatory system and low blood volume due to water loss. Symptoms of heat exhaustion include weakness; dizziness; collapse; headache; weak, rapid pulse; cold, clammy skin; and dilated pupils. The victim of heat exhaustion usually has a near-normal body temperature and continues to sweat. If you experience any of these symptoms while walking in hot weather, move to a cool place, rest, and drink plenty of water.

Heatstroke, also called sunstroke, is the most serious heat-related illness and requires immediate medical attention. Heatstroke occurs when the body cannot get rid of heat fast enough. The body's cooling system is overwhelmed and simply breaks down. Sweating usually stops, the circulatory system is strained, and body temperature can rise to 106 degrees Fahrenheit or more. If immediate steps to cool the victim aren't taken, body temperature will continue to rise and the victim will die. Symptoms of heatstroke include hot, dry skin; rapid pulse; high body temperature; headache; dizziness; abdominal cramps; and delirium. Often, however, the first visible sign of heatstroke is loss of consciousness. Heatstroke is a medical emergency. Immediate steps must be taken to decrease the victim's body temperature. The victim should be moved to a cool area and placed in an ice-water bath or covered with ice packs until medical treatment is available.

There are a variety of steps you can take to protect yourself from heat illness. The cornerstone of prevention is water. If you intend to exercise in hot weather, you need to drink plenty of water before, during, and after your walks. You should drink 2 or 3 cups of cold water about 10 to 20 minutes before you begin walking. During your walk, drink at least a couple more cups of cold water. When you finish walking, drink more water. Don't rely on thirst to tell you when to drink; it's not always an adequate guide to your body's need for fluid.

Another important preventive measure is to slow down your pace and intensity when the temperature is high, especially during the first few days of a hot spell. By walking for a shorter time at a lower intensity early on, you'll give your body a chance to adjust its cooling mechanism to the heat.

During hot weather, you should schedule your walking workouts for the coolest part of the day—early morning or evening. Avoid walking late in the morning or during the afternoon when the sun's rays are most powerful. Also, try walking in shaded areas, such as parks, forest preserves, and tree-lined streets. If there's a breeze, walk with the breeze at your back during the first half of your walk. Then, for the second half of your workout, when you're hot and sweaty, walk into the breeze.

Proper clothing can also help you beat the heat. In hot, humid weather, wear as little as you can. Choose breathable fabrics that will allow your sweat to evaporate. Cotton is a wise choice because it absorbs perspiration and allows sweat to evaporate. For the lower part of your body, try light cotton shorts. If chafing is a problem, spread a little petroleum jelly on your skin in the affected areas. For your upper body, wear a loose-fitting T-shirt or tank top, or try a fishnet vest that lets air in and out. Also, be sure to choose light colors that reflect the sun's rays.

Of course, there is no shortage of expensive fashions. Many walkers wear jogging outfits, which are available in various materials and designs. If you want to wear a jogging suit, make sure to get one that is made of a porous material. In warm or hot weather, you don't want heat and moisture to be trapped; you want it to circulate and escape to keep your body cool. So your warm-weather walking outfit should be made of either cotton or a combination of cotton and a porous synthetic fiber, and it should fit loosely without getting in your way.

Whatever you do, shun rubber, plastic, or otherwise nonporous sweatsuits. They create a hot, humid environment and interfere with the evaporation of sweat. Wearing them makes you an easy target for dehydration, heat exhaustion, and heatstroke. Those who imagine that these clothes will help them slim down are deluding themselves. They may perspire more than someone walking in shorts and lose more water weight while they walk, but they will promptly regain that lost weight as soon as they rush to the water fountain.

When you dress for hot, sunny weather, don't forget to cover your head. The head is the first part of the body struck by the powerful rays of the sun. By protecting your head, you can help control your body temperature when you walk. A lightweight, light-colored cap can help reflect the sun's rays. You may even want to try soaking it in cold water before you put it on.

To protect your skin from the sun's burning rays and help ward off skin cancer, be sure to apply a strong sunscreen to all exposed areas of your skin. This is especially important if you have fair skin. Choose a sunscreen with a Sun Protection Factor (SPF) of 15 or more. You may even want to try a waterproof sunscreen, since you'll be sweating quite a bit.

Perhaps your most important protection against heat illness is knowing when to slow down and when to get inside. Regardless of your physical condition, you need to take into account more than the temperature of the air. As mentioned earlier, humidity can greatly decrease your body's ability to maintain a proper temperature.

Humidity makes the temperature feel hotter than it actually is. The accompanying Heat Index chart tells you the "apparent temperature"—how hot it feels to the average person—for various combinations of air temperature and relative humidity. For example, when the air tem-

Heat Index

"Apparent temperature" refers to how hot it feels when both relative humidity and air temperature are considered. When apparent temperature is between 80 and 90 degrees Fahrenheit, you're likely to fatigue easily when walking outdoors; between 90 and 105, heat cramps and heat exhaustion are possible; over 105, heat exhaustion and sunstroke are likely.

Apparent Temperature (°F)

AIR TEMPERATURE (°F)	0	5	10	15	20	25	30	35	40	45	50	55	60	65	70	75	80	85	90	95	100
115	103	107	111	115	120	127	135	143	151												
110	99	102	105	108	112	117	123	130	137	143	150										
105	95	97	100	102	105	109	113	118	123	129	135	142	149								
100	91	93	95	97	99	101	104	107	110	115	120	126	132	138	144						
95	87	88	90	91	93	94	96	98	101	104	107	110	114	119	124	130	136				
90	83	84	85	86	87	88	90	91	93	95	96	98	100	102	106	109	113	117	122		
85	78	79	80	81	82	83	84	85	86	87	88	89	90	91	93	95	97	99	102	105	108
80	73	74	75	76	77	77	78	79	79	80	81	81	82	83	85	86	86	87	88	89	91
75	69	69	70	71	72	72	73	73	74	74	75	75	76	76	77	77	78	78	79	79	80
70	64	64	65	65	66	66	67	67	68	68	69	69	70	70	70	70	71	71	71	71	72

RELATIVE HUMIDITY (%)

perature is 85 degrees Fahrenheit and the relative humidity is 75 percent, it actually feels like it's 95 degrees Fahrenheit outside. You can find out the air temperature and the humidity level on any given day from local weather forecasts.

When the *apparent* temperature is between 80 and 90 degrees Fahrenheit, you need to use caution when exercising outside. This is especially true if you are just starting a walking program; if you are obese; if you have any serious health problems; if you take medication; or if you are over 50. Under these conditions, you may need to cut down the amount of time you spend walking to avoid fatigue.

When the *apparent* temperature reaches 90 to 105 degrees Fahrenheit, heat cramps, heat exhaustion, and heatstroke are possible if you exercise intensely outdoors. Decrease the intensity and length of your workouts, walk in a shaded area, and be sure to drink plenty of fluids.

When the *apparent* temperature exceeds 105 degrees Fahrenheit, exercising outdoors is dangerous. Heat cramps, heat exhaustion, and even heatstroke are likely. Move your walking program indoors under such conditions.

All of this takes care of walking in Atlanta in July. But what about Chicago in February?

When It's Cold Outside

When the snow starts to fall and the temperature drops, it's easy to slip into inactivity and hibernate like a bear—but don't do it. Keeping up your walking program in winter will help you maintain your fitness level. Getting out of the house can also make you feel better and help you fight off the winter blues, known as seasonal affective disorder or SAD. So try to make it outdoors at least once a day for a walk. Be sure, however, to prepare yourself for the frigid temperatures before you step out the door.

Low temperatures and high winds pose the greatest threats to the cold-weather walker. The *windchill factor* tells you how cold the combination of low temperature and wind feels. Your own motion as you walk increases the windchill factor. If you don't protect yourself adequately from cold and wind, you run the risk of developing frostbite or hypothermia.

Frostbite is the partial freezing of a part of the body. Ice crystals can form within and between the cells in skin, tendons, muscles, and even bones. Frostbite is caused by overexposure to below-freezing temperatures. The extremities—hands, feet, ears, and face—are most vulnerable because your body decreases blood flow to these areas in order to keep your vital organs and muscles warm. These areas are also the ones most often left unprotected. The risk of frostbite is higher in heavy smokers, because nicotine causes constriction of blood vessels in the extremities. Without enough blood warming them, the hands and feet are set up for frostbite.

Signs of frostbite include pain and numbness, a white or blue discoloration of the skin, and loss of function in the affected area. Proper treatment of frostbite involves prompt, careful rewarming. The victim should be moved to a warm area, if possible. The frostbitten area should then be placed in lukewarm—not hot—water. Frostbitten skin should not be rubbed or massaged, as this can cause further damage to tissues. Contrary to popular belief, rubbing frostbitten skin with snow is not useful and can be damaging to the skin. Intense heat, from radiators, stoves, or hot water, should not be used since this may burn the numb skin.

Hypothermia is a condition in which body temperature falls well below the normal temperature of 98.6 degrees Fahrenheit. It's caused by prolonged exposure to cold. The first signs of hypothermia are severe shivering, slurred speech, and difficulty in walking. When body temperature falls below 90 degrees Fahrenheit, shivering usually stops and the patient may be confused or may lapse into unconsciousness. If emergency measures aren't taken to warm the victim, cardiac arrest and death may occur.

Basic treatment for hypothermia is gradual rewarming of the victim. The rewarming must be done gradually to prevent the sudden enlargement of blood vessels at the surface of the body, which may divert too much blood from vital organs. Medical help should always be obtained for a person with hypothermia. While waiting for help to arrive, the victim should be moved to a warm place, covered with blankets, and, if alert, offered a warm, non-alcoholic beverage. Alcoholic beverages should not be given because they tend to reduce body heat. Rubbing the victim's hands or feet to restore warmth is also not recommended.

You can avoid cold-related ailments by protecting yourself and by using caution when the temperature drops and the wind kicks up. The accompanying Windchill Index chart tells you how cold it feels when both temperature (as shown on a thermometer) and wind speed are taken into account. For example, a thermometer reading of 30 degrees Fahrenheit combined with a 25 mile-per-hour wind is equivalent to a temperature of zero when the wind is calm. (The chart shows wind speeds up to 40 miles per hour only; wind speeds greater than 40 miles per hour have little additional affect on how cold it feels.) You can find out both temperature and wind speed from local weather forecasts.

Windchill Index

The "windchill factor" refers to how cold it feels when both temperature and wind speed are considered. When the windchill falls in the left portion of the chart, there's little danger for a properly clothed walker; in the middle section, there's increasing danger of frostbite to exposed skin; in the right portion, great danger.

Temperature/Actual Thermometer Reading (° F)

Wind Speed (mph)	40	35	30	25	20	15	10	5	0	–5	–10	–15	–20	–25	–30
Calm	40	35	30	25	20	15	10	5	0	–5	–10	–15	–20	–25	–30
5	37	33	27	21	16	12	6	1	–5	–11	–15	–20	–26	–31	–35
10	28	21	16	9	4	–2	–9	–15	–21	–27	–33	–38	–46	–52	–58
15	22	16	11	1	–5	–11	–18	–25	–36	–40	–45	–51	–58	–65	–70
20	18	12	3	–4	–10	–17	–25	–32	–39	–46	–53	–60	–67	–76	–81
25	16	7	0	–7	–15	–22	–29	–37	–44	–52	–59	–67	–74	–83	–89
30	13	5	–2	–11	–18	–26	–33	–41	–48	–56	–63	–70	–79	–87	–94
35	11	3	–4	–13	–20	–27	–35	–43	–49	–60	–67	–72	–82	–90	–98
40	10	1	–6	–15	–21	–29	–37	–45	–53	–62	–69	–76	–85	–94	–101

Little Danger

Danger

Great Danger

Windchill Factor/Equivalent Temperature (° F)

The chart also shows you when exposed skin is in danger of freezing. If the windchill factor (equivalent temperature) falls in the section on the left, there is little danger for the properly clothed walker. The middle section shows that exposed skin is in danger of freezing. When the windchill factor falls in this range, you need to cover all exposed areas and watch carefully for signs of cold injury. If the windchill factor falls in the area at the far right, walk indoors.

When dressing for cold weather, simply reverse your hot-weather strategy. Instead of wearing light-colored clothing that reflects the sun's rays, choose dark-colored clothing that absorbs them. If you'll be walking in the evening or early morning, however, be sure to use reflective tape or a reflective vest so that motorists will be able to see you.

In addition, you need to construct a personal heating system that uses your body as the furnace. To do that, dress in layers of warm, loose-fitting clothing. The loose fit allows freedom of movement and promotes comfort. The layering strategy is very much like the insulation in your home; it keeps the heat in and the cold out. The layers of clothing trap warm air and hold it next to your body. The more you work, the warmer the air becomes. At the same time, these layers of warm air act as a barrier to the cold. When it comes to dressing for cold weather, it's the total thickness of the layers, rather than the heaviness of each garment, that really pays off.

The best choices for the innermost layer are polypropylene, silk, or thin, fine wool, because these materials "wick" the perspiration away from your skin. The middle layers should be made of knitted wool or synthetic pile. For the outer shell, use a windbreaker made of water-repellant, tightly woven material that "breathes." A breathable fabric will allow the water vapor from your perspiration to escape, preventing that soggy feeling. Be sure that the seams of the garment are thoroughly sealed to prevent leakage. Male walkers should also wear an extra pair of shorts in extremely cold weather to keep vital areas warm.

After a little practice, you will quickly learn what you'll need for protection from the cold and wind. When you walk in cold weather, it is always better to wear too many layers, rather than too few. That way, you can strip off layers, one by one, as your body heats up. You can then tie this extra clothing around your waist. Even better, however, are outer layers that have a zipper front. This way you can simply unzip the top layers to let air in when you get too hot. As a general rule, you will need slightly lighter clothes than the temperatures might indicate, because you'll be walking, and your walking workout will warm you up to some extent.

Exercise can induce overheating even in winter, although it's much more of a problem in summer. In warm weather, however, walkers tend to be on the lookout for signs of overheating. By exercising continuously for over half an hour, you can raise your body temperature significantly, even if it's cold outside—but cold-weather walkers may not realize this. That's why you need to shed or unzip one or two outer layers as soon as you start feeling too warm.

It's even possible to get dehydrated in the winter, so it's important to drink plenty of fluids before, during, and after your winter walks. Cold acts as a diuretic, encouraging urination and fluid loss from the body. Out in the dry, cold air, you may lose more body fluid than you realize. Your thirst reflex is also depressed in the cold, so you can't rely on it, alone, to tell you when to drink.

In addition to covering your body's core in layers of clothing, it is also important to protect your hands, feet, face, and head, which are most vulnerable to frostbite. Your feet are more susceptible to frostbite when they're wet as well as cold. You're also more likely to get blisters if your socks and shoes get soaked. In cold, wet weather, leather shoes are better than nylon or canvas ones, because they keep your feet drier. You can even put plastic bags over your socks. That may seem absurd, but it has enabled people to walk in snow with suede shoes for over 10 hours without ever getting their socks wet.

It's also important to wear socks when walking. Socks should be made of materials that absorb moisture well, such as cotton or wool. Some walkers prefer cotton to wool, especially for the layer that touches their skin, because wool can be irritating. Whatever your choice in socks, make sure your shoes are large enough to provide plenty of space around your toes. This space will fill with warm air that will insulate your feet nicely and ward off frostbite of the toes.

Some people like to wear two pairs of socks, especially in cold weather. That's fine as long as your walking shoes are big enough to accommodate the bulk of the extra sock. If you wear two pairs of socks and try to stuff your feet into walking shoes that are too small, there won't be enough room for an insulating layer of warm air and you'll be more likely to develop a host of foot problems such as blisters and corns (see Chapter 10). The inner pair of socks should be lighter in weight than the outer pair. Don't select nylon as the lighter, inner sock, because nylon socks tend to promote the formation of blisters.

There are three basic lengths of socks: anklets that reach just above the shoe top, socks that go halfway up the calf, and knee socks. Knee socks and the calf-high variety are more suited for winter walking, because they offer greater protection.

It has been estimated that a hat or cap can hold in 80 percent of the body's heat in cold weather. Without a hat, you lose more heat through your head than through any other part of your body. Put a cap on your head and, in effect, you've "capped" the heat's escape route. In fact, as more than one walker has remarked, "If you want to keep your feet warm, wear a hat." When the weather is really nippy, make sure to keep your ears covered, because the ears are sensitive to low temperatures and can become frostbitten easily. If your hat doesn't cover your ears, try using a pair of earmuffs in addition to the hat.

You may want to try wearing a heavy knitted wool or orlon ski cap that you can pull down over your ears and face. This design gives you flexibility. It can protect you from the cold and be conveniently rolled up to form a cap if you don't want to cover your face.

Many people feel the pull-down mask is the only way to go. When the wind is at your back, you can roll it up and expose your face to the sun's warm rays. When you are heading into a strong wind, you can pull it down over your face to protect your skin from frostbite. A mask can be a mixed blessing, however. Perspiration and condensation of the breath can freeze into ice around your mouth and nostrils—not the most pleasant winter experience. Some walkers have complained that a mask tends to congest the sinuses because it inhibits breathing. Nevertheless, for safety's sake, it may be a good idea to use a ski mask when the windchill factor is low.

Mittens, not gloves, give your hands the best protection in cold weather. They're worth the sacrifice in dexterity. Snuggled together in a mitten, your fingers help keep each other warm. Some people use tube socks as mittens, because they go well up the arm. In really cold weather, some walkers wear mittens with socks on top— or gloves covered by mittens.

Cold weather is no reason to pack away your sunscreen. It's true that sunlight is weaker in the winter, but the ultraviolet rays that burn skin and raise the risk of developing certain types of skin cancer are still around. Especially if it is snowy and sunny, the reflected rays can burn your exposed skin, so it pays to apply sunscreen to all your exposed skin. If you use strong protection in the summer—that is, SPF 15 or higher—then use it in the winter, too. Alcohol-based sunscreens can add to the drying effects of the cold and wind and they don't stand up to perspiration as well as creamy ones do.

If you are driving to an out-of-the-way area to do your cold-weather walking, make sure you toss an extra set of warm clothing and a blanket into the back seat of the car. This should be a regular emergency precaution—like the spare tire in the trunk. You might also want to bring a thermos filled with a hot beverage.

If you do venture out in extremely cold weather, particularly if you're planning a long walk, it is wise to arrange to go with a walking companion. That way, you can each watch out for signs of hypothermia in the other person. It's also a good idea to let someone at home know where you plan to walk and what time you plan to return, especially if it's very cold or if it's snowing.

Just as it is dangerous to drink and drive, it can be dangerous to drink and walk in winter. The reason is that alcohol dilates the blood vessels in your extremities, redirecting blood away from your vital organs and toward your face, feet, and hands. This gives you a dangerous illusion of warmth, when in reality precious heat is being pulled from your vital organs. Alcohol also suppresses the natural shivering mechanism that helps generate heat. Like any other drug that impairs your judgment, alcohol can give you a false sense of well-being. You may literally forget when to come in from the cold.

Cold Weather and Health Problems

Cold weather shouldn't present any serious problems if you protect yourself and are in reasonably good condition. If you have heart problems, however, ask your doctor if it is all right for you to brave cold weather—even if he or she has already given your walking program the go-ahead. The reason for this precaution is that the body's reactions to low temperatures put stress on the cardiovascular system. These reactions include constriction of blood vessels in the skin, shallow breathing through the mouth, and slight thickening of the blood, all of which can lead indirectly to angina (chest pain) in people with heart disease.

In fact, one standard test for heart disease takes advantage of this link between cold and chest pain. In the cold pressor test, the palm of the hand is cooled in water, prompting chest pain in people with hardening of the arteries, but not in others.

Exercising in the cold can be double trouble for people with heart disease. Cold lowers the heart's supply of blood, while exertion raises the demand for it. This imbalance between supply and demand can cause attacks of chest pain. If you have heart trouble, your doctor can give you advice on how to minimize adverse effects of cold on your heart and when to do your walking indoors.

Even in people who don't have heart disease, cold exposure can raise blood pressure. To conserve heat, the muscles contract to obstruct the flow of blood to the arms and legs. This reroutes extra blood to the vital organs and boosts the blood pressure. People who have high blood pressure, therefore, need to take extra care in dressing warmly for cold-weather walks.

Asthma is another condition that can worsen in the winter. Inhaling cold, dry, winter air can trigger bronchospasms—contractions of the air passages in the lungs. To avoid this, many doctors advise their asthmatic patients to take their anti-asthma medications just before they exert themselves in cold weather, according to Peyton Eggleston, M.D., an associate professor of pediatrics at the Johns Hopkins University School of Medicine in Baltimore. If you have asthma, see your doctor before you walk in cold weather.

Also at special risk in the cold are people with Raynaud's phenomenon, which often accompanies connective tissue diseases such as scleroderma and lupus. Cold causes spasms in their blood vessels, which cut off the circulation to their fingers and toes and turn their skin a "chalky" color. These people are advised to exercise indoors during cold weather.

Other Weather Hazards

Rain, snow, ice, hail, lightning, strong winds, fog, and other harsh weather conditions can curtail your outdoor walking. So can high altitudes and darkness. With a little bit of ingenuity, however, you may be able to walk your way around these hazards.

On warm days (temperatures above 70 degrees Fahrenheit), rain shouldn't be much of a problem as long as you keep your feet dry. On rainy days when the mercury dips below 70 degrees Fahrenheit, a light rain jacket will give you sufficient protection. The best materials are waterproof but breathable—that is, they don't let water in, but they do let out water vapor from perspiration. If you don't want to get your hair wet, you can either wear a hat or carry an umbrella.

Some people love to walk in the snow. To cope with the snow, simply follow the directions for walking in the cold (outlined earlier in this chapter). Be sure, however, to wear proper footwear to avoid slipping. Your pace will be slower, but that's okay. If the snow is deep, you'll be working just as hard as you would be at a faster pace on a clean street. If you doubt that, check your pulse.

Walking on the ice can be treacherous. It is easy to slip and injure yourself. If there is ice on the road or sidewalk, it's best to wait until later in the day, when it's been sanded, salted, or melted by the sun. If you can't do that, try to find a clean path. If that is impossible, you may want to walk inside that day, instead.

Hail can be a problem. If the hail is large, take shelter immediately. If it's small, be your own judge. Most of the time, it won't harm you. As soon as you hear thunder or see any lightning, however, head indoors. Walking during a thunderstorm can be dangerous.

If you're walking into a stiff breeze, you may want to slow down. Walking against the wind is like walking through deep snow. It takes extra work, so you'll get the same benefits that you would in a faster walk under normal circumstances.

High altitudes are a source of special problems. At 5,000 feet above sea level and higher, the air contains significantly less oxygen than it does at lower altitudes. So there is less for your body to take in. As a result, your heart has to work extra hard. For every 2,500 feet that you ascend, plan on taking at least a week to adjust to the decline in oxygen concentration. One way that you might adjust is to cut the pace or duration of your program by 50 percent at the beginning. If you find yourself short of breath even at that rate, slow down further.

When the weather turns foggy, follow all the guidelines for walking in darkness (presented in Chapter 12), with one exception. Don't wear white, gray, or other light-colored clothes. Motorists will not be able to see you. Bright red or orange clothing is best.

Chapter 12

FINDING ROOM TO ROAM

One of walking's great advantages is that you can do it almost anywhere. To find a place to walk, all you have to do is step outside your door. By varying the paths you choose to take, however, you can make walking that much more pleasurable—and practical.

Regular, frequent walks provide an ideal opportunity to explore the area in which you live. Each walk can be an adventure, a chance to experience what's going on around you. Try to keep finding new places to walk, because by varying your routine you will help keep up your interest in your walking program. Even brisk walking affords you a good look at the sights around you. You can see the seasons change—and treat yourself to all sorts of sights, sounds, and smells that you would have missed if you had been zipping by in a car.

Where you choose to walk is up to you. The range of choices obviously is unlimited—at least as far as space is concerned. Maybe you're lucky enough to live in an area, town, or city that offers not just walking space—every area has that—but different kinds of space to make your walks as interesting as possible.

Comparisons of Surfaces

When you choose a route, pay close attention to the surface. A lot of walkers say grass or packed dirt is the very best surface for walking. These surfaces are soft, so they are good for shock absorption. Ideally, the surface should be smooth enough to allow you to walk as fast as you want without tripping or twisting an ankle. If the grass or dirt is too clumpy, it won't provide good enough traction and you may stumble or fall. So you'll need to check out the area before you begin a serious walk.

With a little exploration, you can usually find some strip of grass or other unpaved surface on which you can walk. Walking on a sandy beach is very enjoyable. You can even do it barefoot—but you need to watch out for sharp shells or other debris. Walking on soft sand or dirt can increase the energy you expend—and the calories you burn—by as much as one third. It also provides the muscles in the feet with more of a workout, particularly if you walk barefoot.

If you can't find a soft, springy surface to use, pavement is an alternative. One good thing about pavement is that you don't have to travel far to find it. But it does have its drawbacks. Most foot and leg problems are either caused or aggravated by walking on hard surfaces like concrete or asphalt. Wearing good, shock-absorbing walking shoes can help you avoid this problem. Remember that asphalt tends to absorb more heat than concrete, so it can make your feet hotter during warm-weather walks.

Hills and Stairs

Walking up hills and stairs burns extra calories and raises your heart rate more than freestyle walking at the same speed on a flat surface. Thus, it does an even better job of helping you to control your weight and build your aerobic capacity. It also provides more of a workout for the large muscles in the buttocks and the muscles in the front of the thighs, which are responsible for lifting the legs, climbing, and pushing off.

With the heightened benefits of walking on hills and stairs, however, comes an increase in your risk of injury. Some simple adjustments in your walking technique, however, can help you hold down this risk. For instance, while walking uphill, walk slightly slower, lean forward, and swing your arms more vigorously to increase your climbing power. Downhill walking is even harder on the bones and joints, and its high impact forces can aggravate joint problems and cause muscle soreness. To minimize the shock of the downhill landing forces, shorten the length of your stride.

If you have trouble finding stairs or hills that you can climb, you may be able to find a device called a stair-climbing simulator at a local gym or health club.

Cities, Suburbs, and Beyond

The ideal outdoor walking route is a course with a smooth, soft surface that doesn't intersect with traffic. For that reason, parks make excellent walking territory for urban dwellers. Parks often offer soft surfaces like grass and packed dirt to walk on. In addition, they are often secluded from traffic's noise and toxic emissions. Even in parks that have roads cutting through them, there may be designated times when cars are banned and walkers, joggers, and bicyclists rule the road. A prime example is Central Park in New York City, which has enjoyed car-free weekends for much of the past two decades. If it's allowed, you might also try walking along the perimeter of a local public golf course. You'll need to stay alert for stray golf balls, though.

There's another thing you can do to have an enjoyable walk, even if you're not surrounded by trees, grass, and fresh air. Find an old residential neighborhood with beautiful houses or historic buildings that can occupy your attention while you walk. Some historic areas even offer guided walking tours. Be sure that you don't get carried away by the sights, however, and neglect to watch where you're going.

If you walk in an urban area, try to stay away from traffic lights and congested areas. A lot of stop-and-go walking can cause you to lose momentum and break your stride. It can also decrease the aerobic benefits you get from your walks by allowing your heart rate to drop out of your target range. If your urban or suburban route is dotted with traffic lights, however, don't just stand still when the light is red. Instead, try walking in place until it turns green and you can go forward again. This will keep your heart rate up while you wait.

If you live in a rural area, you'll probably have a wider selection of peaceful, grassy walking routes. Paths that border rivers and streams or encircle lakes can make pleasant walking routes, as long as they're not too muddy or slippery. If you follow a narrow rural road, however, you'll need to stay alert for ditches and fast-approaching vehicles. If you choose a field or hilly area, watch out for holes, stumps, and other stumbling blocks. Be sure to read the safety section at the end of this chapter, especially if you'll be walking in the evening or early morning when lack of light can be a hazard.

Mall Walking

Some cities, endeavoring to bring their declining downtown areas back to life, have created outdoor walking malls by banning cars from certain shopping streets. These outdoor malls give you the opportunity to windowshop or run errands while you walk—without having to worry about traffic. (Be careful not to stop walking too often or for too long, however, because you'll lose momentum and decrease the aerobic benefits of your walks.)

Even more common, though, are enclosed shopping malls that cater to walkers by lengthening their hours. Some even let walkers in before dawn or during holidays when all the stores are closed. Many malls now have walking programs sponsored by the American Heart Association. Some have collaborated with local hospitals or health organizations to establish walkers' clubs that provide awards for walking certain distances, discounts for shopping at the mall, occasional free breakfasts, and mileage logs for members. Some malls even offer measured walking courses, so walkers can calculate precisely how far they've gone. Also available in some malls are walkers' maps, fitness seminars, health screening (for blood pressure, for instance), and special stations with instructions for stretching and calisthenic exercises.

Mall walking has many advantages. It gets you out of the house but protects you from the safety hazards, inconveniences, weather extremes, and air pollutants that you might have to struggle with if you did all your walking outdoors.

Malls tend to be conveniently located and safe. Their climates—temperature and humidity—tend to be controlled and kept in a comfortable range. Thus, malls play a major role in promoting all-weather fitness. They offer real protection from the possible adverse health effects of walking in extremely cold or hot weather, a concern particularly for people with heart disease. Often, pollen and air pollutants from traffic are filtered out of the air in malls, offering welcome respite to people who suffer from allergies or pulmonary problems.

Malls that have become popular spots for walkers offer yet another advantage. They turn walking into a sociable activity. Even if you arrive at the mall alone, you'll probably be able to meet other walkers there. Eventually, you may have a large group of walking companions, at least some of whom will be there each time you visit the mall. This kind of peer support can provide crucial motivation to keep you walking.

Of course, the advantages are reciprocal: Walkers don't just benefit from malls; malls glean benefits from walkers. Many mall managers realize that public services such as walking programs are a good way to get people to come to the mall. Walkers help increase mall traffic and frequently patronize mall stores. If you're interested in mall walking but can't find a mall near you that offers a program, you might try contacting a local mall manager to discuss these reciprocal benefits and set up a program.

Gymnasiums and Health Clubs

Many gymnasiums and health clubs feature indoor tracks, treadmills, and even stair-climbing simulators that you can use to move your walking program forward when poor weather or safety concerns force you to cancel your outdoor walk. This setting also offers you an excellent opportunity to integrate your walking program with weight training, aerobics, dance, swimming, and other physical activities.

Indoor/Outdoor Tracks

Walking around and around the same track can be boring. If you are trying to walk a mile, it may take you 20 or more laps. Your mind can grow numb, and it is easy to become discouraged. You can help fight this by walking with a companion, by walking to music, or by mentally organizing your schedule or planning your day as you walk.

If you are going to walk on an indoor track for several days or more, it is best to switch direction every day—for instance, walk clockwise on Monday and counterclockwise on Tuesday. By walking clockwise one day and counterclockwise the next, you will help avoid orthopedic problems that can result from continually rounding corners in the same direction. This is particularly important if the track you're walking on is banked (slanted), because the leg on the down side will be subjected to extra stress.

Treadmills

Treadmills are not just for running or jogging. They are also good for walking. Essentially, a treadmill is a conveyor belt that is designed to allow you to walk or jog in a confined space. There are two kinds of treadmills: motorized and nonmotorized.

Walking on a motorized treadmill is as close to real walking as you can get without actually hitting the street or track. You simulate your natural freestyle walk almost exactly. In motorized treadmills, an electric motor rotates the conveyor belt (sometimes called a walking bed) under your feet, forcing you to walk at a set speed (the speed can be adjusted). The walking bed of many motorized treadmills can be raised at one end to simulate walking uphill, making the exercise that much more difficult and thus increasing its aerobic value. This is an especially useful feature for people who are in such good shape that they need to walk uphill to get their heart rates well into their target zones.

Perhaps most important, a motorized treadmill allows you to walk for precise distances at exactly measured speeds. This is particularly important if you need to monitor your fitness plan carefully or want to keep precise track of your speed. Some motorized models have mechanisms that adjust speed in small increments—one-tenth of a mile or less—so that you don't have to jump from a gait that is much too slow to one that is far too fast.

When you walk on a nonmotorized treadmill, your legs do the work of rotating the walking bed. Compared to motorized treadmills, nonmotorized ones are usually lighter and more compact. Nonmotorized treadmills can also be adjusted so that the resistance against the running bed is higher, or lower, making the workout more, or less, strenuous. Unlike motorized treadmills, they do not allow precise predetermination of the speed at which the running bed rotates, so you may have some trouble keeping track of your pace from one workout to the next.

Walking on a nonmotorized treadmill also tends to be less comfortable than walking on a motorized one. When you use a motorized treadmill your legs propel you forward just as in normal walking. When you walk on a nonmotorized model, on the other hand, your legs push the running bed backwards. Nonmotorized treadmills can be uncomfortable and difficult to work for the long periods recommended for aerobic conditioning—30 minutes or more. The belt is on rollers, and after a period of walking, exercisers may experience a "hot foot" because of the built-up friction. Walking on a nonmotorized treadmill is fine if you're going at a slow to moderate pace, but it can lead to foot and leg irritation at a fast pace.

Many gyms and health clubs have treadmills that you can walk on. The price of a motorized treadmill—even a smaller model designed for use at home—puts it out of reach for all but the most plush home gyms. Most motorized treadmills designed for home use cost over $2,000, with prices as high as $7,000 for some models. Nonmotorized treadmills are generally less expensive. Their prices start at about $600.

Regardless of which type you choose, a home treadmill is a sizable investment. So if you decide to purchase one, it's a good idea to try it out in the store before you put any money down. Walking beds vary in length from one model to another, so make sure the bed is long enough to accommodate your natural stride.

Safety

As you discover new and different places to walk, always consider safety. Traffic must always be taken into account. Particularly if you have to walk directly on the street instead of on the sidewalk, you need to stay alert and watch out for vehicles. Even if you wear reflective strips on your clothing, you may not be seen by a motorist. So walk as you drive—defensively.

A special type of mask has been designed to filter the polluted air many people in urban areas must breathe. If you must walk near cars and trucks that spew out carbon monoxide and other noxious fumes, a mask of this type might make breathing easier.

Even when you have a nice trail available, and traffic isn't a problem, you may still have to look out for bicycles. If you have to share a trail with cyclists, you need to watch out for these two-wheeled vehicles. Collisions can cause serious injuries.

In addition, some city areas are just not safe enough to walk through—certainly not after dark. The best way to protect yourself against these possible dangers is to avoid these areas. If you're planning on walking an unfamiliar route, you may want to drive through it first to check it out. If you find that you've walked into a dangerous area, try to carry your body aggressively, walking briskly and purposefully to an area where you will feel safer. Look like you know where you're going, even if you don't. A person who looks lost is an easy target of street crime.

There are also some things to watch out for if you plan to walk in the countryside. Make sure you're not trespassing. Also, be careful that you don't get carried away by the beauties of nature and the music of the birds—and get lost. Many adventurous walkers like to take along a pocket compass for just such a possibility.

Wherever you go, be sure to watch out for dogs—the well-known scourge of walkers, joggers, and mail carriers. If you encounter a dog, try not to look scared. Just walk away from it slowly. Do not stare at the dog. If the dog looks as if it's going to charge at you, shout "down" in a stern, angry tone; this should scare the dog off. If the dog does attack, lift your knee up to prevent the dog's progress and hit the dog in the snout with a stick, rock, or your arm. If you've been bitten by a dog, seek immediate medical care.

For safety's sake, if you listen to an audiocassette or radio as you walk, make sure to keep the volume low enough so you can hear what's going on around you. Listen and watch for cars, bicycles, and other pedestrians, especially when you're turning a corner.

When walking at night, follow these basic guidelines:

1. Face the traffic as you walk, and stay close to the edge of the road. If a car seems to be bearing down on you, step off the road and stop walking.

2. Wear light-colored clothes. White is best. You might also try wearing reflective tape or a reflective belt or vest.

3. Carry a flashlight so you can see where you're walking; the light will also alert motorists to your presence.

4. Try to avoid walking on any road at night before you've had a chance to get familiar with the road during the day. By checking out the road during daylight hours, you'll know where the curves and ditches are.

5. Don't look directly at the headlights of oncoming cars. They tend to blind you, and as a result you can't see where you are going. Instead, look off to the side. You'll still be able to see the car with your peripheral (side) vision.

Chapter 13

FINDING TIME FOR FITNESS

You're convinced, right? We've succeeded in talking you into beginning a walking program and getting yourself into shape. You've explored new places to walk and found plenty of room to roam. You've checked up on your health, figured out your target heart rate, and chosen the program that's right for you. That's great.

However, if you're like many people with busy schedules and sedentary jobs who know they ought to be more active, you may already be wondering how long you'll be able to stay with your walking program. Maybe you're asking yourself: "How long will it be before I lose interest, am sidetracked by an extra-busy time at work, or invent any number of other excuses for not walking?"

Don't let these worries keep you from starting to walk. Begin now, and refer to this book whenever you feel the need for another dose of encouragement. In this chapter and the next, you'll find suggestions for sticking with your walking program. This chapter focuses on fitting fitness into your schedule—not only in terms of finding time to walk, but in terms of making regular walking a priority in your life. In the next chapter, we show you how to vary your walking routine so that your walks continue to be enjoyable.

The Dropout Problem

When it comes to getting health benefits from physical activity, your ability to stay with a regular exercise program for life is even more important than the intensity of the activity itself. Unfortunately, figuring out how to get people to take up exercise and integrate it into their lifestyles permanently hasn't proved all that easy for exercise scientists.

Despite the fruits of years of research on exercise compliance, nearly 50 percent of people who begin a supervised exercise program drop out within 6 months to a year, according to Rod K. Dishman, Ph.D., associate professor in the department of physical education and director of the Behavioral Fitness Laboratory at the University of Georgia, in Athens. The dropout rate is the same regardless of whether people exercise in community and work-site fitness programs, in programs to prevent first and second heart attacks, or in outpatient programs for the treatment of overweight, diabetes, or depression. Even many patients referred to an exercise program by their doctor or hospital never show up for the first session.

Dr. Dishman suggests that one reason for this apparent inability to translate research on exercise compliance into lower dropout rates in real-life programs may be that exercise is a unique behavior. In other words, it may not be subject to exactly the same reinforcements—or "carrots" and "sticks"—as are other health habits. Exercise also demands more time and effort than do many other health-promoting behaviors, like brushing your teeth or having your blood pressure checked. The knowledge that exercise can provide health benefits may help people get motivated to *begin* an exercise program. However, their continued involvement over the long haul appears to depend much more on positive reinforcement from friends, family, and health professionals, and on a sense of well-being and achievement.

Dr. Dishman suggests, however, that attention should not be focused solely on whether people drop out of *supervised* exercise programs or continue attending them. The reason is that many people who have dropped out of such a program—and many who have never even enrolled in such a program—may be pursuing long-term physical activity on their own. Self-motivated people are particularly likely to keep up a long-term exercise routine without any supervision. So they shouldn't be considered dropouts from physical activity. Walking is a prime example of an activity that is easily pursued in just such an unprogrammed fashion.

Instead of concentrating too much on official exercise programs, Dr. Dishman advises, more attention should be paid to motivating the estimated 65 percent of the American population who are sedentary. These are the people who stand to benefit most from adding more physical activity to their lives. They're also the people who are more likely to begin and stick with a less strenuous activity such as walking.

Studies of exercise compliance have identified convenience as a major factor. People who drop out of exercise programs tend to live farther away from the exercise site than do those who stick with it. Convenience is one reason why walking has such a low dropout rate as a lifelong activity. Walking really can be incorporated into your daily routine, no matter how crammed full of sedentary duties it is. Compared with an exercise class at a health club, for instance, following your own personal walking program is cheaper in terms of both money and time. In addition, although you may enjoy walking with a friend or family member, walking is something you can do on your own as well. So you can set your own walking schedule, without having to wait for your partner or team to show up, as you would have to do for many other activities.

Building Walking into Your Life

You can build walking into your life in a variety of ways. One convenient method is by turning everyday errands and chores into opportunities to walk. Taking your dog for a brisk, 30-minute walk, for instance, can provide both you and your pet with a hearty workout. If you need to take clothes to the dry cleaner, try choosing one that's a mile or two from your home and walk the distance instead of driving. If you have a baby at home, break out the baby carriage and go for a lengthy, moderately paced stroll that can lull baby to sleep and give you an aerobic workout.

If you need to go to the shopping mall to pick up a few things, try parking at the far end of the lot and walking to the door—or better yet, choose a mall that's within walking distance and leave your car at home. Once you're inside, take a quick trip or two up and down the length of the mall before you begin shopping. After you've purchased everything that you need, take another couple of brisk laps around the mall (as you walk, you may even remember something that you forgot to purchase).

If you work at a sedentary job all day, try walking during your lunch hour, as well as to and from work. If you have to attend meetings and appointments outside of the office, use them as another chance to walk. Such a work-day break can clear your head and help you prepare for the meetings.

Whether you work on the second floor or the tenth, try walking up the stairs instead of taking the elevator to your office. This can help tone the muscles in your legs and buttocks and help you burn calories even if you have only a couple of flights to climb. If you work on one of the top floors in a skyscraper, try getting off the elevator several floors before yours and take the stairs the rest of the way. Work-site studies have shown that workers who simply began using staircases in favor of elevators and escalators improved their overall physical fitness by 10 to 15 percent.

Even when you have to spend hours at your desk or computer terminal, you can practice an essential part of your walking fitness program. You can do stretches frequently throughout the day to maintain your flexibility. (The more flexible you are, the less chance you'll have of injuring yourself when you take your walks.) Stretching can also help to relieve tension and wake you up. You don't need to change clothes or leave your work area to do many of these stretches. You can do head rolls, shoulder shrugs, leg lifts, and ankle twirls while you're seated. Then, when it comes time for a coffee or restroom break, you can stand up and stretch your legs. If possible, visit a coffee machine or restroom that's on a different floor, so you can use, the stairs to get there and back.

If you have to go on a business trip, there's no reason to suspend your walking program. If possible, ask your travel agent to book you into a hotel within walking distance of your appointments. That way, you can get to know a new city as you make your brisk way from your hotel to your appointments. If your travel plans include lengthy layovers at airports, pack your walking shoes and use the time to walk.

You can use your imagination to come up with new ways to build walking into your daily routine. Keep in mind, however, that to make great gains in aerobic fitness, you need to walk continuously for at least 30 minutes at your target heart rate. Making too many stops and starts during your walks allows your heart rate to fall and prevents you from achieving an aerobic training effect. That's not to say that you shouldn't try to walk at every opportunity you get. As discussed in previous chapters, any activity that you can do above and beyond your regular walking workouts can provide additional health benefits.

The key to fitting fitness into your schedule is to not take the easy way out and succumb at every opportunity to every time-saving modern invention designed to keep us from walking. The subliminal message we get from being constantly surrounded by all these inventions is that walking is something we should avoid. But as this book explains, walking is actually good for you and worth incorporating into your life at every opportunity. So the next time you find yourself driving around the parking lot looking for that space up front, think about the benefits of walking. Then head to the far end of the lot, park your car, and walk.

The Walking Commuter

Many walkers have managed to work their walking program into their daily commute to and from work. They're proof of what we've been saying throughout this book: Walking is the easiest of all exercises to build into your routine. Walking to and from work may take a little longer than commuting in a car, bus, or train, but the rewards are well worth it.

If you must drive or travel by public transportation for many miles to get to work each day, you might assume that there's no way you can walk to work. You can't walk the entire distance, that's true. But you *can* try parking a manageable distance from work and walking the rest of the way. If you take public transportation, on the other hand, you can try getting off the bus or train one or two stops early and walking the remaining distance.

If you drive to work, you might save money and even time if you walk part of the way. As many long-distance commuters know only too well, the longest part of the drive to work is often the last mile or two, as you near the congested area that everyone is converging upon. If you're really unlucky, it can take the last ten minutes of an hour-long drive just to go the last four blocks. If you parked your car four, six, or eight blocks from work, you could probably walk that distance in the same amount of time it takes you to drive, fight for a parking space, and get to your office. You might even beat your driving time by walking that last bit of the trip. Chances are you'll also pay less for parking, because you won't be fighting for a prime parking space. Depending on the location, if you play your cards right, you may even be able to find a free space.

Corporate Programs

Many corporations have taken up the idea of a corporate fitness program that stresses walking. Some of these programs involve a brisk two- to four-mile walk, with warm-up and cool-down sessions, during lunch hours. An increasing number of employers are realizing that they can make an important contribution to their employees' welfare and productivity simply by encouraging them, through financial and physical incentives, to walk to work, at least part-way.

If your employer hasn't jumped on the bandwagon, you might try bringing up the idea. Here's one idea that deserves consideration: The company could rent parking lots a mile or two away from its offices, so employees could park there and walk to work. In case of bad weather, umbrellas could be placed at the office and parking lots for use by the walking employees. This system has the built-in potential for progress checks and rewards. Some sort of sign-in or sign-out procedure could be used to check whether employees use the facility. Many companies are already awarding their physically fit employees with special financial incentives. This system would lend itself perfectly to such a program.

The chief financial officers of some companies may read this suggestion and think, "Terrific. But how much is all this walking going to cost, and who's going to pay for it?" In a way, it would be just like any other investment. It might cost a few dollars at first, but that money would quickly pay dividends in terms of healthier, more productive employees who take fewer days off for illness. And it probably wouldn't hurt a company's insurance rates, either. In fact, employee fitness programs are not just an attractive fringe benefit but also a profitable investment for the company. Such programs have been shown to result in decreased absenteeism, reduced health care costs, and increased productivity.

Corporate leaders are realizing that a walking program can be the simplest and least expensive way to get their employees moving with regular exercise. And regular exercise has been shown to help employees escape everyday office pressures and competition—and become more productive at work.

Walking on the Job

There are some people who don't have to worry too much about fitting fitness into their schedule. They may not need to concentrate so hard on building walking into their commuting or their lunch hours. These are the ones for whom walking is actually an integral component of their work.

Examples include waiters, waitresses, ushers, meter readers, litter collectors, caddies, and policemen on the beat. Some of the most conspicuous working walkers are mail carriers, whose lower rate of heart disease, compared with sedentary postal clerks, was discussed in Chapter 2. If you walk a lot on your job, pay attention to how often you stop. If you don't walk continuously, you may not be getting much of an aerobic training effect, so you may want to schedule regular, vigorous walks outside of work to build your fitness.

The Proper Attitude

When you're trying to fit walking into your lifestyle, having the proper attitude can make all the difference in the world. After all, you're not as likely to find time to exercise if you look at it simply as a chore. In this section, you'll find some simple steps you can follow to make exercise a natural, convenient, and enjoyable part of your routine.

STEP ONE: Set a goal. Goals are important in life. They give you something specific to work toward and a way to measure your progress. When you're setting a goal, avoid vague generalizations like these: "I want to get into shape," or "I want to lose weight." Instead, set precise, long-term, intermediate, and short-term goals.

For instance, if you want to lose weight, find out what your ideal weight is and decide how much weight you want to lose in six months or a year. If you want to lose 20 pounds during that period, that is your long-term goal. Your short-term goal might be three pounds by the end of the first month. (Your intermediate goal would be somewhere in between.)

What kind of goals should you set? Take stock of yourself right now. What would you like to achieve? Whatever it is, write it down. Even if it seems unrealistic at this time, put it on a sheet of paper or a card and save it. This is your long-term goal. Once a week, you can take out the sheet of paper, write down your progress, and make a note of anything that seems to be preventing you from achieving your goal.

Next, you need to plan how you are going to reach your goals. Write down your plan, and be specific. For instance, how many additional minutes of walking are you going to do each week to get to your long-term goal?

Finally, make a note of what you'll do today—not tomorrow, but today. Write down how long, at what time, and where you're going to walk.

STEP TWO: Record your progress. For some people, the thing that makes sports like football, basketball, and baseball so endlessly fascinating is the competition. If competition really gets you moving, you can get it from racewalking—or even from competing against yourself. Just use a progress chart, which will tell you how well you're doing and how close you're coming to your goal. Charting your progress can give you the sense of achievement that helps keep exercisers motivated.

The chart doesn't have to be complicated. The simplest chart is just a regular calendar on which you write the information about your walking progress. Many people record their mileage on a map. Your regular walking route may take you around the same section of your neighborhood every day, but you can mark off your distance on a map as though you were walking cross-country. By the end of a year, you may find that you've walked a distance equal to that between San Francisco and San Diego—or between New York and Miami. This helps in setting long-term goals, too. For instance, you can promise yourself that by the end of the year, you'll have walked the same number of miles as you would had you walked from Chicago to Houston.

STEP THREE: Set a workout time. Have you ever noticed how easily you slip into routines? Perhaps you always brush your teeth before, not after, you shower in the morning; always put your left, not your right, shoe on first; or always take the same route to work every day. And have you ever noticed how you tend to feel you've forgotten to do something important if anything should interfere with one of these rituals? You may find it easy to stay with a walking program if you can allow it to become part of your daily routine—so much a part that you'll feel compelled to walk despite your own excuses for skipping a day. If you can get yourself into the habit of walking at a certain time every day, you'll accept it as part of your regular daily schedule and not just something to do during your "free time."

Whatever you do, don't worry about taking the time. You may have coworkers who think nothing of taking a two-hour, three-martini lunch. They may cast a scornful eye at you as you go off to take your regular lunch-hour walk. But you'll be doing something positive for your body, and it will make you feel better and more alive. You'll certainly be more productive in the afternoon than you would have been after even one martini.

Many people feel they can't find the time in their busy schedules to exercise. But exercise, including walking, need not take much time, especially compared with the amount of time most Americans spend watching television. It's simply a matter of priorities. Others may get so tired out by their work and their responsibilities at home that they feel they have no leftover energy with which to exercise. This can become a vicious cycle, however, because the more out of shape you are, the more easily you will get tired out. To break the cycle, make time for walking and stick with it. You'll find you have more energy and feel less tired.

STEP FOUR: Choose the best time of day. The best time depends on you. It's important, however, to schedule your walking workouts for a time when you are least likely to have to cancel or interrupt them because of conflicting demands from work or home.

Some walkers like to venture out early in the morning, some even before daybreak. They like the solitude available at that hour, when the streets are still empty of traffic and people. They can slowly get their minds and bodies going and do a little thinking in the silence. And if they are walking where they can see the horizon, they can savor the exhilarating sight of dawn.

Even some walkers who are decidedly not morning people—the types who ordinarily just drag themselves around till noon—swear by an early-morning walk. They say their morning walks give them a "jump start" on the day, making them feel more alert and energetic on the job. By the time they sit down at their desks, they feel invigorated enough to tackle any work that comes their way.

Lunch hours are an increasingly popular time for regular, vigorous walks. Some people walk for the first 45 minutes of their lunch hour and grab a bite during the last 15 minutes. Walking at lunchtime gets them out of the office (or house) and into a refreshing midday break. If you want to follow your walking program during your lunch hours, however, be sure your lunch hours are long enough to accommodate the times specified in your walking program.

Other walkers wait until they have left their work, put their jobs behind them, and headed home. A walk at this time provides a nice transition for them, a time to work off some of the day's tensions so that they don't have to carry them into family life.

Late evening seems to appeal to some people as the best time. You might want to take a couple of factors into account, however, before you set late evening as your walking time. When you put walking as the last item on your agenda for the day, it often gets treated that way—last. You may tend to put other things in place of it or skip it because you don't have enough time or energy left. Also, some people find that a walk right before bedtime revs up their metabolism so much that they have difficulty falling asleep. On the other hand, some people find that a walk in the late evening can help them relax and unwind enough to fall asleep. So you may want to experiment with walking at this time first before you decide to make it a habit.

STEP FIVE: Dress the part. If possible, have a special outfit and wear it only for walking. Anything comfortable—an old pair of shorts or jeans and a sweatshirt, for instance—will do. How you look is not the point; it's how you feel. In changing from regular clothes into a "walking outfit," you can "psych yourself up" for the activity. In effect, you're telling yourself you mean business and really intend to collect all the rewards that are coming to you from walking. Be sure, however, that your outfit is appropriate for weather conditions.

STEP SIX: Think the part. What happens in your head is almost as important as what happens to your body. If you don't enjoy what you're doing, you'll begin to find reasons for not doing it.

Before you walk, try to get yourself into a positive, active frame of mind. As you walk, be aware of what's happening to your body. Feel your muscles work. Concentrate on the rhythmic flow of your movements. Walking can be a very pleasurable sensory experience.

STEP SEVEN: Walk with others. If you're married, your spouse has to be on your side. A study conducted at the Heart Disease and Stroke Control Program bears this out. Men in an exercise program did one hour of physical activity three times a week for eight months. The men whose wives encouraged their participation had good attendance in the program; those whose wives were neutral or had negative feelings about the exercise had a much poorer attendance record. The conclusion: The spouse's attitude was critical. So if you can, try encouraging your spouse to join you in your walking program or begin one of his or her own. You'll not only be increasing your chances of sticking with your program, you'll be encouraging your spouse to increase his or her fitness and health.

Walking with a friend can also give you the advantage of companionship and encouragement. In an investigation conducted at the University of Toronto, scientists reported a greater dropout rate for individual exercise programs than for group programs. Only 47 percent of those on individual programs were still active at 28 weeks, compared with 82 percent of those in the group programs. If you think your motivation is weak—or weakening—walk with a partner or with several friends. (For more on using the "buddy system" in your walking routine, see Chapter 14.)

STEP EIGHT: Walk tall. Don't worry about what other people think. As you're walking down the street, you may think that everyone is looking at you. Chances are that no one will pay any attention. If somebody does stare, so what? You're doing something good for your body; they're not. Besides, they may simply be admiring your ambition.

Chapter 14

SPICING UP YOUR ROUTINE

The first step in establishing walking as a lifelong activity is to incorporate it into your everyday routine. Even if you've managed to build walking into your life, however, you may still need to add boredom-busting variations to your walking workouts to keep yourself from joining the all-too-ample ranks of the exercise dropouts. Variety is the spice of life. So whatever it takes to add variety to your walking routine, do it; it will help keep you committed to walking for a lifetime and make each walk more enjoyable than the last.

The novelty doesn't need to be as unusual as walking on stilts to do the trick (although some people do enjoy stilt-walking). It can be walking to music, walking with a friend or your family, taking a walking vacation, joining a walking club, participating in walking events, or adding other activities to your walking program. You may even want to try setting a walking record.

Walking to Music

Walking to music is an excellent way to spice up your walking routine and keep up your momentum at the same time. Walking to music can also help you get your mind off pressures and problems so that you can concentrate on your walking instead. Portable radios and tape players, handily equipped with headphones, make it possible for you to take your music with you as you walk.

A variety of audiotapes, specifically designed for walkers, is now available. These tapes feature music with a beat that closely matches the rhythm of a brisk walk. Some tapes are divided into three sequences: music for warming up, music for maintaining a heart rate fast enough to condition the heart and lungs, and music for cooling down. The beat helps you keep your pace, with the tempo starting out slowly, building gradually, then finally slowing down again, bit by bit. You can, of course, create your own tape using favorite tunes. Try to select music that has a clear beat to help you keep your rhythm.

Enjoy the music, but don't get too carried away. For the sake of safety, you still need to stay aware of your surroundings. It's a good idea to keep the volume control at a sensible level—not blasting—so you can hear any danger signals around you, such as honking car horns, shouting people, or barking dogs.

The Buddy System

For many people, a daily, solitary walk is a welcome opportunity to be alone, to reflect on the events of the previous day or the day ahead, and to sort out their thoughts. Walking, however, can also be a sociable activity. Even if you're breathing deeply, you can still chat with a walking companion. As a matter of fact, walking with a companion is a good way to take the "talk test" (see Chapter 4) to be sure you're not walking too fast. Moderate-paced walking shouldn't leave you breathless, so it's an excellent activity to share with a friend.

The hidden advantage of the "buddy system" is that it helps motivate you to walk. It's a whole lot harder to use an excuse not to walk, like "It's too cold out," or "I'm too busy today," when a friend is waiting for you. Instead of having just one person—yourself—to shoot down your excuses for not walking, you'll have two—yourself and your buddy. It's a reciprocal arrangement: Your buddy can help motivate you to walk when you are feeling lazy, and you can do the same thing when your buddy falls into a similar mood.

Even if you start out walking alone, you may well find plenty of company—and potential walking partners—out there. More and more people are rediscovering the joys of walking.

A Family Affair

One of the best ways to add fun to your walking routine is to make it a family affair. Like walking buddies, family members can boost your motivation—they may be even better at nudging your conscience to keep you in the swing of things when you'd just as soon quit.

One pleasant ritual you may want to introduce your family to is a relaxing evening amble in the twilight, that magic time. Be sure to wait awhile after dinner, however, especially for a brisk walk. It's best to avoid strenuous exercise for at least two hours after eating.

If you're going to add variety to your own routine by making walking a family affair, be sure to bring the kids along. You may think, "I don't have to worry about the kids—they get lots of exercise." It is true that they probably do get more exercise than you and may seem very active—perhaps astoundingly so.

However, consider these questions: How much time do your children (or younger siblings, nieces, nephews, or grandchildren) spend watching television rather than riding their bikes or playing tag? While the kids may attend gym classes at school, are they really participating in aerobic activity? Do your children walk to school or do they ride there in a bus or car?

You're certainly not doing it purposely, to be sure, but you may be bringing up your children to lead sedentary lives. Studies have shown that children mimic their parents' behavior, so if you've been sedentary, then in effect you've probably been teaching your children to be less active.

You also play an important role when it comes to your children's attitudes about television and automobiles. Most kids in the United States spend over three hours each day watching television. If your television is turned on most of the time, your children may learn passive leisure. They may grow up to be "couch potatoes." At some time during each day, you might want to assert yourself as a parent and turn off the television. While the set is off, encourage walking and other physical activities.

As for your car, keep it in the garage and take it out only when trips really call for it. By relying less on your car, you will be teaching your children to build walking permanently into their lives. Some families that have tried this have become so wrapped up in walking that they now proclaim a "no-car day." On that day, no one can use the car except for an emergency.

In far too many schools, the emphasis is placed on athletics for the gifted few, rather than for everyone. To compound the problem, physical education and athletics generally focus on team sports rather than on potentially lifelong activities such as walking. And what's even worse, burnout from participation in school athletics may even discourage future activity. How many times have you seen a coach discipline players by having them run laps or do push-ups as punishment for misbehavior or an error on the playing field? This punitive approach may actually discourage fitness.

In addition to adding variety to your routine, involving your children in your walking program is a great way to set an example for them and encourage them to develop and maintain physical fitness for the rest of their lives. Walking with your children also provides an opportunity for extra talking, sharing, and learning.

There's another advantage to walking as a family. Often, it's difficult for a family to pick an activity that everyone can do well enough so that everyone gets involved. The family includes people of various ages, shapes, sizes, and levels of physical fitness. Not every family member will have the same skill in skiing, tennis, golf, or basketball. However, even toddlers can walk, and when they get tired, they can be placed in a stroller or baby sling.

Far too often, parents find themselves exasperated when they bring their small children along on a walk. There's no getting around it: The children's legs are shorter, and they will walk slower than you do. They may also want to use the walk as an opportunity for rambling and discovering new things, further slowing down their pace. One solution is to allow more time for each walk, so you can let the children walk at their own pace—and enjoy it yourself. If you have only a limited amount of time for a walk, you can push the child in a stroller.

When walking with the family, make sure to vary your route, even if you merely walk in the opposite direction every other day. You might also encourage the children to invite one or two of their friends along or have them walk the family dog or cat. One more useful variation: Let one of the older children lead another child who shuts his or her eyes. This is an activity that is often used by educators to heighten a child's awareness of his or her surroundings and develop the nonvisual senses. Be sure, however, that you keep an eye on them as they do this. You might also try walking together to go out to dinner, to go shopping, or to go to religious services.

You must emphasize safety. When they walk along a road where there are no sidewalks, children must learn to walk along the left side of the road, against the traffic. (Many walkers have had particularly harrowing experiences when walking on the right side of the road, with the traffic.) Teach your children to walk well to the side of the road and emphasize traffic rules, such as obeying traffic lights and crossing at crosswalks. As in driving, they need to learn to watch out for the other guy.

Finally, make sure the children wear light-colored clothing. If they are wearing dark clothing, have them wear bright arm bands or hats. That way, motorists can see them better.

Will you be able to talk your children into walking with you and staying in a walking program? Yes, provided you set an example yourself, and support your children with positive comments about their growing walking skills. In this way, you'll be able to maximize the health and happiness of your family's future generations. Don't push your children into walking, however. Nagging won't do much good; you'll just turn them off to fitness. Try to encourage an atmosphere of cooperation and togetherness and a sense of adventure. Show them how much you enjoy your walks and they'll be more likely to follow your example.

Walking Vacations

A walking vacation is a great way to add novelty to your walking program. Not only does a walking vacation give you something to plan for, it also gives you a lot to remember. Years after you enjoy a walking tour of Paris, for instance, the early-morning hustle and bustle you encounter as you walk through your own town may remind you of the sights, sounds, and smells of Paris. Suddenly, you'll be transported back in time and place—all in the course of a quite ordinary stroll in your own neighborhood.

Hiking trips are popular examples of walking vacations (see Chapter 8 for more on hiking). There's also an abundance of American cities to choose from, each with its unique parks and neighborhoods to explore. Foreign cities, towns, and countryside also provide delightful territory for walking. Americans travelling abroad often remark on how much more hospitable other countries are to walking. Old World cities, built long before the automobile came to prominence, tend to offer meandering streets and broad, tree-lined boulevards that are ideal for walking.

Some countries also have walking traditions that can be a joy to discover on a walking vacation. One example is Switzerland, whose hills and mountains are crisscrossed with hiking trails. Often, the trails feature stations where the walker can take advantage of instructions and equipment for calisthenic exercises. Another lovely walking tradition is the evening promenade in Spain; whole families converge on central squares to stroll and greet one another.

Your walking tour can be as spartan or luxurious as you choose. You can arrange to spend your nights camping out, or staying in hostels, inns, or hotels—and still spend your days walking. Unless you are an experienced hiker or long-distance walker, you'll want to limit most of your treks to about ten miles per day. If possible, arrange your travel plans so that you can take your time and walk at a comfortable pace.

It can take a lot of preparation to map out a walking tour. Some travel agencies offer pre-arranged walking tours, where your accommodations and your daily walking routes will be mapped out for you. Even if you go on a regular tour, you can try to skip the cabs and tour buses and walk to your destinations.

Carrying all the guidebooks, maps, and brochures you need to steer you in your walking vacations can be a weighty proposition. To relieve this burden, some enterprising companies are marketing walking tour guides on lightweight audiocassette tapes. Check with the tourist bureau at your destination, too. They may have prepared tour tapes that you can borrow, rent, or buy.

Walking Clubs

You may want to take a step beyond just walking with friends and family—and join a walking club. Clubs are springing up all over the country.

Many clubs sponsor walking events, which certainly can put some zip into your walking program. These events range from low-key togetherness walks to high-powered racing events. On the friendlier, noncompetitive end of the spectrum are 6- or 12-mile walking events called volkswalks—that's "people's walk" in German—sponsored by local branches of the American Volkssport Association. Many worthy charities also sponsor walking events. (See the appendix for more on walking events.) Remember, too, that many racewalkers—and freestyle walkers—join events that are meant primarily for joggers. Marathons are an example: Covering 26 miles is no mean feat, whether you jog, racewalk, or just plain walk it. Be sure that you prepare for these events; gradually increase the distance of your daily walks before you enter a long-distance event.

Cross-Training

Cross-training means devoting oneself to more than one activity for fitness. By definition, it's a boredom buster, because you can switch from one activity to another. If you've been following a walking program, and you now feel that you're ready for a new challenge, cross-training may be for you.

For walkers, cross-training is an important opportunity to choose a companion activity that does what walking doesn't do—that is, build upper-body strength. Swimming and weight training are activities that can build upper-body strength. The same goes for rowing and cross-country skiing—and for the equivalents of these activities performed on exercise machines.

You can devise your own personal cross-training routine, using walking as the cornerstone of your active lifestyle. Start by choosing just one new activity and do it on "off" days when you don't do your fitness walking. Keep in mind that, just as in walking, you need to progress with your companion activity gradually. After adding one activity on top of your regular walking routine, wait at least three months before adding yet another activity.

"There's a promising future for cross-training," says Dr. James Rippe of the University of Massachusetts, who is both a walker and a jogger himself. "And walking is going to be one of those things that is increasingly used in cross-training." He notes that more and more top athletes—including runners and triathletes—are using brisk walking for their cross-training. The reason is that brisk walking and running use different muscles, so walking allows the athlete to work on strengthening those different muscles and developing flexibility.

Going for the Record

The walkers who've earned a place in the record books, achieving amazing walking feats, provide an important source of inspiration for continuing your own walking program—and possibly for considering building up to attempt such a feat yourself. Here are just a few inspiring examples from the annals of walking:

► Robert Sweetgall completed a 11,208-mile solo walk and lecture tour that took him through 50 states in 50 weeks. Seven times during the walk, which was sponsored by the Rockport Company, he was flown back to the University of Massachusetts Medical Center, where Dr. Rippe and his colleagues conducted exhaustive medical tests on him. It became the most comprehensive scientific testing ever performed on the long-range effects of walking on an endurance athlete. The researchers found that Sweetgall's oxygen consumption rose during the walk. By the end, it was over 20 percent greater than that of the average man of his age, height, and weight.

► Jesse Casteñeda, a native of Mexico who lives in Albuquerque, New Mexico, keeps breaking walking records while raising funds for humanitarian causes. In 1973, he became the first person ever to walk 300 miles (equivalent to the distance from Boston to Philadelphia) without stopping. He covered 302 miles in 102 hours and 59 minutes, with no breaks for sleeping—only the occasional break to use the bathroom in the trailer that came along to support him. In

1982, he walked across the country, from New York to California. He wasn't trying to break any record that time, but it took him a brief four-and-a-half months, averaging 35.2 miles a day, even with 2 days off per week spent meeting local people, visiting hospitals, and giving guest lectures. Before that, Casteñeda broke the men's record for distance walked in 24 hours: He covered 142 miles and 448 yards.

► Journalist Steven Newman, who lives in Ohio, completed the first documented solo walk around the earth. In his worldwalk, he walked more than 21,000 miles across 20 countries on five continents. The trip, which took 1,460 days, was achieved without any commercial sponsors or grants. Newman relied on the kindness of strangers the world over for sustenance.

► David Kwan started out in Singapore on May 4, 1957, and walked all the way to London in 81 weeks. Kwan averaged 32 miles a day and passed through 14 countries during his 18,500-mile trek.

► Plennie L. Wingo covered only 8,000 miles—a mere stroll compared to Kwan's long-distance achievement—but Wingo is in the record books. Why? Because Wingo walked backward the whole way. He wore special glasses that enabled him to see where he was going. Wingo started his journey in Santa Monica, California, on April 15, 1931; he arrived at his destination of Istanbul, Turkey on October 24, 1932. Forty-five years later, at the age of 81, Wingo decided to celebrate the anniversary of his transcontinental backward walk by walking backward from Santa Monica, California, to San Francisco. He covered the 452 miles in 85 days.

Chapter 15

SHOES AND ACCESSORIES

We've said before that walking doesn't require much in the way of equipment. One of the only—and by far the most important—items that you'll need is a pair of sturdy, comfortable walking shoes. If you don't take time and care in selecting your shoes, you may be in for some serious discomfort. In addition to walking shoes, there are a variety of accessories available that can increase your comfort, safety, and enjoyment as you walk. As you progress through your walking program, you may want to add them to your walking gear.

What to Look for in Shoes

As walking has gained popularity as a form of exercise, a wide variety of shoes meant specifically for walking has appeared on the market. The unique designs and features of many of these shoes have evolved from research into the mechanics of walking. This research has shown that the stresses put on the feet in walking are different from those exerted in other exercises such as jogging, tennis, and aerobics. If you walk, it makes good sense to select shoes designed specifically with walking in mind, according to Dr. James Rippe of the University of Massachusetts Medical School.

True, many walkers used running shoes when walking was a less popular fitness activity and running shoes dominated the market. Now, however, you have a wide variety of well-constructed walking shoes to choose from. These shoes are more suitable for walking than are running shoes because running shoes tend to have more cushioning and less stability than walkers need.

Recently, a few shoe manufacturers have come out with all-purpose "workout" shoes that are supposed to be adequate for people who walk a little, run a bit, and play sports, too. By definition, however, such shoes won't be as good for walking as a shoe that is made specifically to accommodate the unique biomechanics of walking, according to William A. Grana, M.D., secretary of the American Orthopedic Society for Sports Medicine. Nor can such a shoe really protect against the stresses of running, tennis (with its side-to-side movements), or basketball (with its risk of twisted ankles). Therefore, to protect your feet and provide them with the cushioning and support they need as you walk, your best bet is to go with walking shoes.

When you shop for walking shoes (as with any other type of shoes), you'll want to find a pair that fits your feet. The basic shape of the shoe should conform to the shape of your foot, and the *toe box* (the area around your toes) should be high enough, wide enough, and long enough to accommodate your toes comfortably. (See Chapter 10 for more information on fitting walking

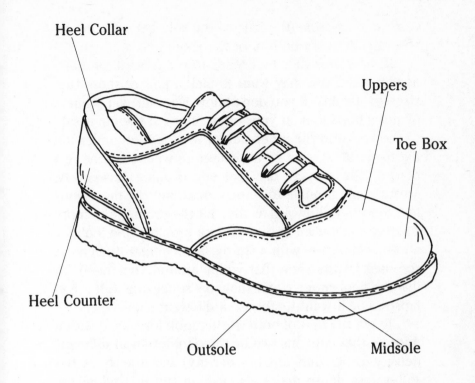

Heel Collar

Uppers

Toe Box

Heel Counter

Outsole

Midsole

shoes to prevent discomfort and injury.) The fit isn't the only factor to consider, however.

You'll want to find shoes that cushion and support your feet as they hit the ground with each walking step. Shoe design, however, often involves a trade-off between cushioning and stability. A well-cushioned shoe may not control the foot's motion adequately. An extremely rigid shoe, on the other hand, may not provide the shock absorption and flexibility necessary for comfort.

If you have had stress fractures (see Chapter 10), joint problems, or back pain in the past, you may want to opt for a shoe that stresses cushioning over stability. You'll want a shoe that has a well-cushioned *insole* (the shock-absorbing lining inside the shoe, upon which your foot rests) and *midsole* (the part of the sole between the insole and the very bottom of the shoe).

If, however, your foot tends to roll inward (pronate) as you walk, you may want to pick a pair of shoes that stresses stability. If you don't know whether you pronate or not, take a look at your other shoes. If the outer side of the heel and the inner side of the forefoot (under the big toe joint) show a great deal more wear than the rest of the sole, chances are that you pronate excessively. Most people pronate to some extent, but the more your feet tend to roll inward as they hit the ground, the more support you'll want to prevent foot problems. So look for a more rigid shoe with a sturdy *heel counter* (the cup at the back of the shoe that wraps around your heel). To test the heel counter of a shoe, try squeezing it. If it collapses, you'll want to choose a different shoe.

To get the best of both worlds, look for a shoe with a midsole that contains two or three materials of different density (called dual or triple density). In these shoes, the softer, less dense materials cushion the feet while the firmer, denser materials stabilize the feet and make the shoes more durable. You may also want a shoe that has a *heel cup*, a padded, cup-like area inside the back of the shoe that cushions the heel *and* holds it in place.

The sole of the shoe should be flexible at the ball of the foot. If you can bend the shoe in the middle (below the arch support), however, you won't get enough arch support and your feet may tire easily. The *outsole* (the very bottom of the sole that comes in contact with the ground) should be made of a durable, springy material like rubber yet should be soft enough so that if you press your fingernail into it you can see an indentation. The outsole should also be patterned to provide traction.

Some walking shoes have a "rocker" sole—that is, they are thicker under the ball of the foot than are other types of athletic shoes, and they curve upward in front. This design helps support the foot as the body's weight is transferred from the heel to the toe.

Instead of the flat-bottomed sole found in running shoes, some walking shoes feature a distinct heel (as shown in accompanying illustration). This type of walking shoe may be a good choice for people who are prone to developing aching arches, midfoot pain (plantar fasciitis), and heel spurs (see Chapter 10).

The *uppers* (the part of the shoe above the sole that covers the feet) should be made of soft material that "breathes," allowing sweat to evaporate. Leather, or a combination of leather and nylon, provide good support for the feet. The uppers should have a padded *heel collar* (the part of the upper surrounding the opening of shoe) and tongue. Some shoes feature a notched heel collar that helps prevent irritation of the Achilles tendon.

Your choice of uppers—and style—will rely, in part, on where and when you'll be doing most of your walking. If you walk a great deal at work—or on your way to and from work—for instance, you may want to check out some of the new, dressier styles of walking shoes. If you'll be doing a lot of walking on uneven ground, such as grass or gravel, you may want to look into high-topped walking shoes that will protect your ankles.

When you shop for walking shoes, take your time. Examine each shoe carefully. Run your fingers along the inside of the upper to be sure there are no protruding seams that can cause blisters in the toe area. Poke your fingers into the insole and the heel area to be sure they're soft yet firm.

When you try on a style, put both shoes on and lace them up. If you'll be wearing two pairs of socks when you walk, wear them both when you try on your shoes. Be sure to walk around in the shoes—on both concrete and carpet. And finally, find out about the return policy on the shoes. Some stores will allow you to return or exchange shoes after a short trial period—as long as you haven't worn them outdoors.

Racewalking Shoes

Unlike fitness walking shoes, racewalking shoes can be harder to find—mainly because there are far fewer styles produced. Designed specifically for maximum speed in competitive racewalking, these shoes are very lightweight. They have less cushioning in the sole and heel than do freestyle walking shoes, however, so unless you're a dedicated, competitive racewalker, stick with a lightweight fitness walking shoe.

Boots for Hiking and Backpacking

If you're going hiking—especially on rugged, uneven terrain—you'll need a pair of boots or shoes that protect and support your feet and ankles. Ideally, hiking boots should have high-top, padded collars that cover your ankles. The soles should be stiff, to protect the bottom of your feet from rocky terrain, and lugged or treaded, to provide good traction.

Another important feature is weight. If you're going on shorter walks, or if you'll be hiking through less rugged terrain, you may be able to get by with a pair of sturdy walking shoes. You might also want to check out the new lightweight nylon hiking boots. They look more like athletic shoes, often weigh half as much as traditional hiking boots, and contain liners made of waterproof, breathable materials.

If you'll be doing a lot of hiking, through all kinds of weather, on rocky, uneven terrain, however, traditional hiking boots are probably your best bet. They're usually made of leather and have thick, heavy soles. They provide the best support and protection, but they're also heavier than the nylon models.

Walking Socks

If you choose them wisely, socks can greatly increase foot comfort and help protect against foot problems as you walk. Good socks for walking need not be designed specifically for this activity. However, they should fit properly. Socks that are too small can cramp your toes and even increase the risk of foot problems, such as hammertoes. On the other hand, socks that are too large can bunch up, rub against your feet, and cause blisters.

The socks you choose should be shaped to fit your feet and should be seamless, since friction can build up between a seam and the skin and promote blisters. They should also be thick enough to help absorb the forces that build up as the heel of the shoe strikes the ground. Often, this thickness is reinforced with a bit of extra padding where you need it most, at the heel and toe.

Walking Sticks

Many walkers—especially those who also hike—like the feel of a walking stick. It helps them keep their rhythm as they walk. Using a walking stick can also increase the involvement of the upper body. On rough terrain, the stick can be used to detect holes and unstable ground. It can also be used to ward off dogs.

Several different types of walking sticks are available. Some are made of lightweight aluminum. Others are solid and made of hard wood. The type of tip you'll want on the bottom of the walking stick will depend on the surface you're walking on. Pointy steel tips are useful for walking on icy surfaces and mountain trails. Plastic tips help keep wooden walking sticks from splintering when they're used on hard surfaces.

Some walking sticks can be broken down into two or three pieces for easy storage. Other models are made of reflective material and therefore serve as a safety device during evening walks. Some walking sticks even have tips that unscrew to reveal handy items like a compass or a sundial. Of course, if you live near a wooded area, you may simply want to choose a piece of fallen wood and use it as a homemade walking stick.

Pedometers

A pedometer is a device that gives an estimate of the distance you travel on foot. It registers the number of steps you take by sensing the body's movements. Most pedometers need to be calibrated—in other words, you have to punch in the length of your stride first. One way to do this is to mark off a 100-foot stretch of level ground. Then as you walk that stretch, count the number of strides you take. When you've reached the end of the marked distance, divide 100 by the number of strides you took and enter the resulting stride length into the pedometer. If you enjoy jogging as well as walking, however, you should be aware that you can't use the same pedometer, set to the same adjustment, to gauge your performance in both activities (that's because your jogging stride will be longer than your walking stride). Instead, you'll either have to get two pedometers, one for walking and the other for jogging, or you'll need to keep adjusting the same pedometer back and forth for the two activities.

Some pedometers attach to your waistband, while others are placed around the wrist. Some are even built into shoes. Some devices can estimate not only your distance but also your average speed, the number of calories you burn, and the amount of time it takes you to walk a certain distance.

Pulse Gauges

Several types of devices are available to measure your pulse as you walk. Some are hand-held, while others are worn on the wrist like a watch. Pulse gauges offer an advantage over manual pulse-taking because they allow you to find out your heart rate *while* you walk, instead of having to stop to count heartbeats. (Remember, your heart rate begins to slow down within 15 seconds of when you stop walking.) Some very elaborate pulse gauges even take advantage of ultrasound technology to measure heart rate.

Portable Radios and Tape Players

Lightweight, portable radios and tape players are popular walking companions. They come in a variety of sizes and styles, from those that attach to your belt to those that are incorporated into headsets. Some headphones are even built into earmuffs—a handy innovation in the winter. Specially made belts are also available with pockets in which you can carry the portable radio or tape player.

Carrying Valuables

Even if you're not going on a day-long hike, you may still need to carry a few things—money, keys, identification—with you as you walk. One popular way to do so is to use a "fanny pack." A fanny pack is a specially made belt with a zippered pouch. The belt can be adjusted so that the pouch area rests in front or in back—whichever is most comfortable. (If you'll be walking in a crowded area, you'll probably want the pouch facing forward for safety's sake.) Some manufacturers even make socks and shoes that come with tiny, sealable pouches for keys and change.

Special packs are also available for carrying infants while you walk. These packs feature a collar to support the baby's head, as well as an inner pouch to position the infant securely. Newborns, who need more support, do best when carried on the chest. The same pack can later be used to carry the older infant on your back.

Water Bottles

From Army-style canteens to high-tech insulated thermoses, a variety of portable containers are on the market for carrying liquid during walks. Some models feature an insulated carrier that keeps the contents of the bottle cool on hot days and warm on cold days. Others have a dual function. They come equipped with a handle so that you can use the filled container as a hand-held weight.

Reflective Gear

Reflective gear is important for your safety when you walk at night, particularly if you are walking along a road in an area with no streetlights or sidewalks. When a car's lights hit the reflective gear, you become visible at a much greater distance than you would be if you wore nonreflective white or light garments. Reflective gear is no absolute guarantee of safety, however, so you'll still need to stay alert and face the traffic as you walk.

Reflective material is incorporated into many garments, including vests, headbands, belts, sashes, and leg bands. You can also purchase reflective safety trim that can be sewn, taped, or ironed onto your walking outfit. Ideally, the reflective gear should be worn on the chest, arms, waist, legs, and ankles. It's especially important to wear reflective material on your legs and ankles, because much of the light from headlights is directed toward the ground, and because these body parts are moving and therefore may attract the driver's attention.

WALKING CLUBS AND EVENTS

Walking Clubs and Organizations

American Mall Walkers Club
P.O. Box 883
Westbury, NY 11590
(send self-addressed, stamped envelope)

American Volkssport Association
1001 Pat Booker Road, Suite 203
Universal City, TX 78148
(512)659-2112

American Walkers Association
6221 Robison Road
Cincinnati, OH 45213

The Athletic Congress (TAC)
(national governing body for racewalking)
P.O. Box 120
Indianapolis, IN 46206
(317)638-9155

North American Racewalking Foundation
P.O. Box 50312
Pasadena, CA 91105
(818)577-2264

Walkers Club of America
P.O. Box 883
Westbury, NY 11590
(send self-addressed, stamped envelope for
information)

Walkers Club of America Training Camp
Box M
Livingston Manor, NY 12758
(send self-addressed, stamped envelope for brochure)

Walkabout International
835 Fifth Avenue
San Diego, CA 92101
(619)231-SHOE

Walking Information Centers

Rockport Walking Institute
(Conducts and commissions research on walking and
its cardiovascular benefits; and disseminates
information on walking through literature, speakers'
bureau, forums, and special events)
P.O. Box 480
Marlboro, MA 01752
(617)485-2090
attention: Debbie Kravetz

The WalkWays Center
(Publishes *WalkWays Newsletter* and *WalkWays
Almanac* and sponsors "WalkWays at Your Doorstep," a
program designed to help individuals and communities
create more nice places to walk in their areas)
733 15th Street, NW, Suite 427
Washington, DC 20005
(202)737-9555

Hiking Clubs and Organizations

American Hiking Society
1015 31st Street, NW
Washington, DC 20007
(703)385-3252

American Youth Hostels
Travel Department
P.O. Box 37613
Washington, DC 20013-7613
(202)783-6161

Appalachian Mountain Club
5 Joy Street
Boston, MA 02108
(617)523-0636

Appalachian Trail Conference
P.O. Box 807
Harper's Ferry, WV 25425
(304)535-6331

British Tourist Authority
40 W. 57th Street
New York, NY 10019
(212)581-4708

Florida Trail Association
P.O. Box 13708
Gainesville, FL 32604
(904)378-8823

Long-Distance Hikers' Association
Cindy Ross—coordinator
Box 194, RD 2
Kempton, PA 19529
(215)756-6995

National Audubon Society
950 Third Avenue
New York, NY 10022
(212)546-9202

National Campers and Hikers Association
4804 Transit Road, Building 2
Depew, NY 14043
(716)668-6242

Sierra Club
730 Polk Street
San Francisco, CA 94109
(415)776-2211

U.S. Orienteering Federation
P.O. Box 1444
Forest Park, GA 30051
(404)363-2110

Wilderness Society
1400 I Street NW
10th Floor
Washington, DC 20005
(202)842-3400

Yellowstone Association
P.O. Box 117
Yellowstone National Park, WY 82190
(307)344-7381

For information on National Park Service facilities for hiking and camping, contact:
Office of Public Affairs
National Park Service
Department of the Interior, Room 3043
Washington, DC 20240
(202)343-7394

For maps of trails throughout the National Park Service, contact:
U.S. Department of Interior
18th and C Streets NW, Room 1013
Washington, DC 20240
(202)343-4747

Events

American Hiking Society Hike-In and Annual Meeting
American Hiking Society
1015 31st Street, NW
Washington, DC 20007
(703)385-3252

Appalachian Long Distance Association Annual Gathering
Long-Distance Hikers' Association
Cindy Ross—coordinator
Box 194, RD 2
Kempton, PA 19529
(215)756-6995

Volkssport Reunion Walk
American Volkssport Association
1001 Pat Booker Road, Suite 203
Universal City, TX 78148
(512)659-2112

Walkabout International 56-mile One-Day Endurance Walk
Walkabout International
835 Fifth Avenue, Suite 407
San Diego, CA 92101
(619)231-SHOE

WalkAmerica
(to raise funds to prevent birth defects)
March of Dimes
Contact your local March of Dimes chapter or
March of Dimes Headquarters
303 South Broadway
Tarrytown, NY 10591
(914)428-7100

Walk with Your Doc
(to raise funds for the American Diabetes Association)
American Diabetes Association
Contact your local American Diabetes Association chapter.

Appendix B

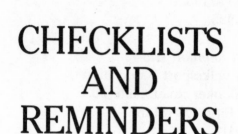

CHECKLISTS
AND
REMINDERS

Taking Your Pulse

There are two main locations for checking your pulse—the carotid artery in your neck (next to your Adam's apple) and the radial artery in your wrist (on the inner side of your wrist, below the heel of your hand).

Use the index and middle fingers of one hand to detect your pulse.

When you've found your pulse, count the number of beats for ten seconds. Then multiply that number by six to find out your heart rate.

You can also try counting your pulse for six seconds and multiplying by ten. Counting for six seconds is especially useful when you're taking your pulse during a walk, because there's less of a chance that your heart rate will slow down before you've gotten an accurate count.

Finding Your Target Heart Rate Range

(USING A PERCENT OF YOUR MAXIMUM HEART RATE*)

STEP ONE: Find your maximum heart rate, either by taking an exercise test or by subtracting your age from 220.

STEP TWO: Multiply your maximum heart rate by .6 (60 percent) to find the lower limit of your target range.

STEP THREE: Multiply your maximum heart rate by .9 (90 percent) to find the upper limit of your target range.

(USING YOUR MAXIMUM HEART RATE RESERVE*)

STEP ONE: Measure your resting heart rate by counting your pulse for ten seconds and multiplying by six. (Do this at rest.)

STEP TWO: Subtract your resting heart rate from your maximum heart rate. (You can find your maximum heart rate by taking an exercise test or by subtracting your age from 220.)

STEP THREE: Multiply the result of STEP TWO by .5 (50 percent) and add that to the result of STEP ONE to find the lower limit of your maximum heart rate reserve target zone.

STEP FOUR: Multiply the result of STEP TWO by .85 (85 percent) and add that to the result of STEP ONE to find the upper limit of your maximum heart rate reserve target zone.

* See Chapter 4 for more detailed information.

Hot Weather Checklist

☐ Drink plenty of cold water before, during, and after walks.

☐ Wear as little clothing as possible.

☐ Choose loose-fitting clothing made of lightweight, breathable fabric. Cotton is a wise choice because it absorbs perspiration and promotes evaporation of sweat. Spread petroleum jelly on areas prone to chafing.

☐ Shun walking outfits made of rubber, plastic, or other non-porous materials.

☐ Choose light-colored clothing to reflect the sun's rays.

☐ Cover your head with a lightweight, light-colored cap. Try soaking it in cold water before putting it on your head.

☐ Wear a waterproof sunscreen with a Sun Protection Factor (SPF) of 15 or more.

☐ Slow down your pace and decrease the intensity of your walk, especially when humidity is high.

☐ Walk in a shaded area such as a park or forest preserve.

☐ Avoid walking in late morning or early afternoon when the sun's rays are strongest; instead, walk in the evening or early morning.

☐ Review the Heat Index chart in Chapter 11 so you'll know when to move your walking program indoors.

Recognizing Heat Injury

Heat cramps
Symptoms of heat cramps are painful muscle spasms, usually in the legs or abdomen, that occur during or after intense exercise. Body temperature is normal or near normal.

The victim of heat cramps should move to a cool area, rest, and sip cold water. The affected muscle should be massaged gently to relieve the cramps.

Heat exhaustion
Symptoms of heat exhaustion include weakness; dizziness; collapse; headache; weak, rapid pulse; cold, clammy, pale skin; heavy sweating; dilated pupils; and normal, or near-normal body temperature.

The victim of heat exhaustion should lay down in a cool area and sip cold water. Victim's clothing should be loosened.

Heatstroke
HEATSTROKE IS A MEDICAL EMERGENCY. IMMEDIATE STEPS TO COOL THE VICTIM MUST BE TAKEN TO AVOID A FATAL OUTCOME.

Symptoms of heatstroke include hot, dry skin; lack of sweating; rapid pulse; abdominal cramps; headache; dizziness; delirium; loss of consciousness; and high body temperature.

The victim should be moved to a cool area and placed in an icewater bath or covered with ice packs until emergency medical treatment is available.

Cold Weather Checklist

☐ Wear dark-colored clothing to absorb the sun's rays.

☐ Dress in warm, loose-fitting layers to trap body heat and keep cold air out.

☐ If you're male, wear an extra pair of shorts to keep the groin area warm.

☐ Top off your layers of clothing with a breathable, waterproof windbreaker.

☐ Unzip or remove outermost layers as you begin to heat up.

☐ Wear a warm hat that covers your ears or wear earmuffs in addition to a hat.

☐ In cold, windy weather, cover all exposed skin to avoid frostbite. A ski mask or scarf can be used to protect the face.

☐ Wear mittens instead of gloves—or on top of gloves—to trap heat around fingers.

☐ Wear calf- or knee-length socks made of absorbent material like cotton or wool.

☐ Wear a waterproof sunscreen on all exposed skin.

☐ Drink plenty of water before, during, and after your walks to avoid dehydration. Do not drink alcoholic beverages before or during your walks.

☐ Review the Windchill Index chart in Chapter 11 so you'll know when to move your walking program indoors.

Recognizing Cold Injury

Frostbite

Signs of frostbite include pain, numbness, and eventual loss of function in the affected area. Frostbitten skin often appears white or blue.

The victim of frostbite should be moved to a warm place. The frostbitten area should be rewarmed gradually and carefully by soaking it in lukewarm—not hot—water. Frostbitten skin should not be massaged or rubbed (especially not with snow). Avoid placing the frostbitten area in or near intense heat, as this may burn the numb skin.

Hypothermia

Symptoms of hypothermia include severe shivering, slurred speech, and difficulty in walking. If body temperature drops below 90 degrees Fahrenheit, shivering may cease and the victim may appear confused or may lapse into unconsciousness. Eventually, cardiac arrest and death can occur if emergency measures aren't taken.

The victim of hypothermia should be moved to a warm area and covered with blankets until medical treatment is available. If the victim is conscious, warm, nonalcoholic beverages should be given. Do not rub the victim's hands or feet.

Nighttime Walking Checklist

☐ Walk on sidewalks whenever possible.

☐ Use extra caution when approaching intersections.

☐ If you must walk in the street, walk on the left side of the roadway, facing traffic.

☐ Wear light-colored—preferably white—clothing.

☐ Wear reflective trim that can be sewn, taped, or ironed onto your walking outfit. Be sure to wear some on your legs and ankles, since they will be moving and may be more likely to catch a motorist's attention.

☐ Carry a flashlight and keep it lighted as you walk to alert motorists of your presence.

☐ Avoid walking on an unfamiliar road or path at night. Check out the road during daylight hours first so you'll be aware of any curves, ditches, or potholes.

☐ Allow your eyes a few minutes to become adjusted to the dark before you actually begin your walk.

☐ Don't look directly at the headlights of oncoming vehicles. Instead, look off to the side and use your peripheral (side) vision to detect vehicles.

☐ If a car seems to be bearing down on you, step off the road and stop walking.

INDEX

neuropathy (nerve damage)
and, 40
nonweight-bearing activities,
and 61
sustaining injury in, 40
Diet
balanced, 62–66
changes in cooking and eating
habits, 65
Dieting
and effects on metabolism, 14,
15
excessive, and effects on
menstrual periods, 41
Digestion, walking's effects on,
43
Dishman, Rod K., 198
Distance, importance of, 36–37
Dogs, coping with, 194
Downhill walking
risk of injury and, 187
strengthening effects of, 21
weight loss and, 19

E
Eggleston, Peyton, 182
Electrical impedance, 20
Electrocardiogram, 60
Emphysema, and Special Starter
. Program, 80
Endorphins, natural pain killers,
56
Endurance, walking and, 29
Energy, increased through
walking, 49–51
Environmental organizations,
hiking and, 110
Everglades National Park, 109
Exercise
dropout rates and, 198–199
for strength, 120–
health benefits of, 31–47
how long to wait after meals,
65
overexertion warning signs,
72–73
programs, goals and, 17–18
reducing cancer risk by, 43–44
self-confidence and, 50, 53,
55–57

weight-bearing, and aging, 46
weight-bearing, and bone
density, 41
what to eat before, 66
Exercises for strength (illustrated)
Arm Arc, 134
Arms Over, 135
Curl-down, 141
Head and Shoulder Curl, 139
Modified Push-up, 136
Regular Push-up, 136
Right Angles, 135
Single Leg Raises, 142
Sit-up, 140
Swing and Bounce, 143
Trunk Twister, 138
Wall Push-up, 137
Exercise test, 60, 67, 70, 83

F
Family, walking with, 215–218
Fanny packs, 234
Fat
as energy source, 18
in daily diet, 62–63, 66
measurements of, 20
vs. muscle, 19–20
Fatigue, chronic, walking and, 50
Fight or flight mechanism and
stress, 52
Flexibility, walking and, 29,
119–120
Fog, walking in, 182–183
Food groups, 63–65
chart, 64
Foot-strike pattern, for walking,
76
Form, in racewalking, 91–96
Fractures, metatarsal stress, 150
walking shoes and, 227
Frisch, Rose, 17, 43
Front Leg Stretch, 126
Frostbite, 173, 178, 179
Fuel, for activity, 18

G
Glycogen, as stored energy
source, 18
Goals
setting, 17–18
walking and 17–18, 56, 205–206

Injuries, increased risk in uphill
and downhill walking, 187
Injury
avoiding, 23, 77
risks of in aerobic dancing, 28
risks of in jogging, 28
risks of in running, 27–28
risks of in walking, 27–29
Insole, for walking shoes, 152,
227
Institute for Aerobics Research in
Dallas, 50, 71
Insulin, 40
and blood sugar level during
activity, 66
International Amateur Athletic
Federation, 91–92

J
Johns Hopkins University School
of Medicine, 182

K
Kwan, David, 223

L
LaPorte, Ronald, 25, 32, 36–37
LDL (cholesterol), 36
Leon, Arthur S.,
Lightning, walking and, 182–183
Lordosis, (sway back) 159
Low density lipoprotein (LDL)
("bad" cholesterol), 36
Lower back stretches, 131
Lower body strength, 29, 104
Lung disease, chronic, walking
and, 40–41
Lupus, cold weather and, 182

M
Mail carriers, walking and, 205
Mall walking, 189–190
allergy sufferers and, 190
heart disease patients and, 190
pulmonary problems and, 190
Marathons, walking and, 221
Mask, for filtering air, 193
Massage
after racewalking, 96
for reducing tension, 54
Mattress, back pain and, 159
Maximum heart rate, calculating
67–68

Maximum heart rate reserve, 69
calculating target zone, 70
for Basic Starter Program, 79
for Basic Walking Program, 81
Mental health, walking and, 47,
49–57
Metabolic rate
exercise, increased alertness
and, 50
weight loss and, 14–19
Metatarsal stress fractures, 150
Midsole, for walking shoes, 227
Multiple Risk Factor Intervention
Trial (MRFIT), 34, 46
Muscle, building, 15
Muscle/fat ratio, 15, 29
Muscles
abdominal, and back pain, 159
cramps and spasms, 156–157
groups, 20–21
soreness and stiffness, 157–158
toned in racewalking, 90
toned in walking, 20–21
wasting, aging and, 45
wasting, dieting without
exercising and, 15
Music, walking to, 214

N
National Institute of Mental
Health (NIMH), 49, 53, 55
National Institutes of Health
consensus panel, 42
National Park Service, 110
Neck Turns stretch, 123
Neuromas, 150
Newman, Steven, 223
Night, guidelines for walking at,
195

O
Obesity, 15
compulsive eating and, 15
high blood pressure and, 38
stress cycle and, 15
Olympic event, racewalking, 90
Opiates, natural, 56
Orthotics, 149, 152, 156
Osteoporosis, walking and, 41
Outsole, for walking sho
Overheating, in winter, 177